Danny,

Many of the things
listed in this book
you already know + do.
It's what makes you
the wonderful guy
you are!

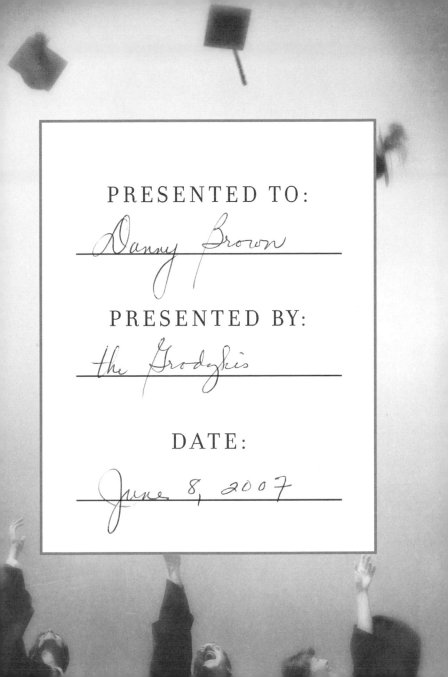

PRESENTED TO:

Danny Brown

PRESENTED BY:

the Grodykis

DATE:

June 8, 2007

Life is a succession of moments.
To live each one is to succeed.

CORITA KENT

101 THINGS YOU SHOULD DO BEFORE YOU GRADUATE

DAVID BORDON AND TOM WINTERS

Faith Words™

New York Boston Nashville

Project developed by Bordon Books, Tulsa, Oklahoma
Concept: David Bordon and Tom Winters
Project Writing: Michelle Medlock Adams, Vicki J. Kuyper, and Rebecca Currington in association with SnapdragonGroup℠ Editorial Services
Cover design: Lookout Design

FaithWords
Hachette Book Group USA
1271 Avenue of the Americas, New York, NY 10020
Visit our Web site at www.warnerfaith.com

Printed in Singapore
First Edition: April 2007
10 9 8 7 6 5 4 3 2 1

The FaithWords name and logo are trademarks of Hachette Book Group USA.

ISBN-10: 0-446-57921-1
ISBN-13: 978-0-446-57921-6:

Introduction

Graduation is a time we all look forward to. It's the culmination of years of hard work and study, whether we are graduating from a much-loved high school, an Ivy League university, a culinary institute, or a hard-earned apprenticeship. The point is you've stayed the course, finished the race, and now you are ready to begin situating yourself for the next step in your journey—postgrad life.

101 Things You Should Do Before You Graduate was written as a reminder not to miss a thing during those pregraduation years, to squeeze every ounce of joy, laughter, insight, and inspiration out of the days ahead, so that you can look back with a smile—no regrets. It's also a reminder that life after graduation will have new challenges—challenges better considered before you find yourself alone in a raft on the big river of life.

Read these pages with care. Revel in the fun and meditate on the wise. Your days are numbered, so make the most of them!

CONTENTS

101 THINGS
YOU SHOULD
DO BEFORE
YOU GRADUATE

1

MAKE EXERCISE A HABIT

Walking—or running—to and from class is typically enough to offset late-night pizza and never-ending soft drinks. But the time is coming when your active lifestyle may find itself crammed behind a computer desk in a tiny cubicle somewhere. By then you may not have the energy or motivation to make exercise a habit. Most people admit that's when they began fighting their own personal battle of the bulge.

Even if you've never been the "fitness type," now is the time to make exercise your friend. After getting your doctor's permission, start off walking for twenty minutes a day. Then, do the jog/walk method—jog a lap, walk a lap, jog a lap, etc. (You get the idea.) Work your way up to three miles and keep at it until it's something you do almost without thinking.

Don't get distracted by focusing on losing weight or timing up or breaking speed records. Instead, focus on finding a comfortable pace and making it part of your mental and physical routine. Remember, the most important factor is that you do it every day. Think of it as an investment in a happy, healthy life.

Experts say that it's hard to beat walking as exercise, but if you just don't find that option attractive, there are many other ways to stay fit. Look into weight training, work out at a local gym, get involved in a sport you can enjoy playing long after you've departed the hallowed halls, or hit a nearby pool. Liking what you're doing will keep your exercise regimen in place when time and energy become precious commodities.

A long, healthy life is God's best for you. Honor Him by making lifelong fitness a priority before you graduate—and after.

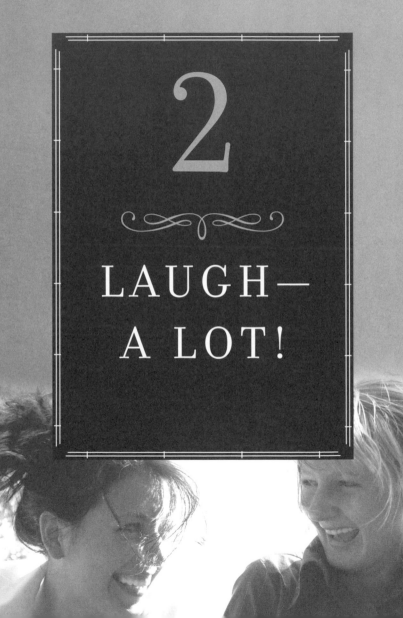

2

LAUGH—A LOT!

L aughter is one of God's greatest gifts to the human race. According to information on the Discover Health Web site, by the time a child reaches nursery school, he or she will laugh about three hundred times a day. How many times a day do you laugh? If you're like most adults, you laugh only about seventeen times a day, and that's just not enough.

We all need to laugh on a regular basis. Proverbs 17:22 says, "A merry heart does good, like medicine" (NKJV). In other words, laughter is good for your body. It actually stimulates circulation, produces a sense of well-being, exercises the face and stomach muscles, stimulates the production of endorphins (the body's natural antidepressants), and provides oxygen to the brain, to name a few benefits.

Want some more reasons to laugh every day?

Giggling is a good workout. Laughter actually burns calories—as many as doing several minutes on a rowing machine. Now, which is more fun—rowing or laughing?

Laughter reduces stress, and what student doesn't encounter stress? Laughter eases muscle tension and psychological stress, keeping the brain alert.

A hearty laugh is good for your heart too. According to a study at the University of Maryland Medical Center, laughter may actually help prevent heart disease. The study found that people with heart disease were 40 percent less likely to laugh in a variety of situations as were people of the same age without heart disease.

In addition, laughter makes you more attractive—that's right! Get started right away. Crack yourself up!

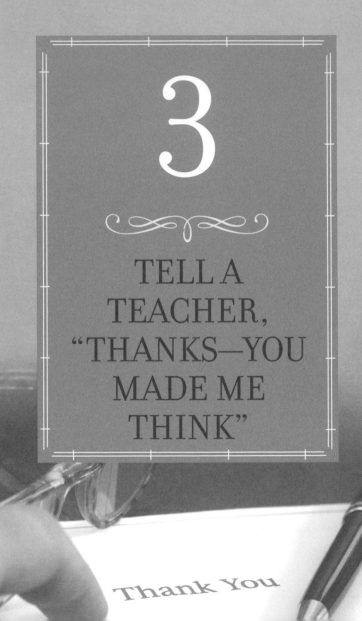

3

TELL A TEACHER, "THANKS—YOU MADE ME THINK"

L et's face it: teaching is, for the most part, a thankless job. It's not every day a student dashes up to a teacher in the hall and says, "Thank you so much for those fabulous, never-ending homework assignments. I've enjoyed them, and I'm a better person for having worked my way through all those piles of reading, writing, and research!" You think? When a teacher does get a "Thank you," it's usually something like—"Hey, thanks for the A!" or even more often: "Thanks for passing me. I really thought I was a goner!"

The thing is that on the other side of graduation, you'll begin to understand that your education consists of more than the grades on your transcript. It's all the little things that led up to those grades— the "aha" moments that came while you were working your way through those endless homework assignments, and the small but significant insights that helped you grow as a person.

In light of that, why not thank your teachers now while you have the opportunity and they can still look out over the classroom and see your smiling, appreciative face? Let them know that you are grateful for the ways they pushed you to dig deep, discard preconceived notions, and open your mind to new cognitive pathways. Say thanks for the grunt work, the repetition, the hard ground you've been asked to plow. Say, "Thanks for teaching me how to use the brain God gave me. Thanks for making me think!"

4

SLOW DANCE WITH SOMEONE SPECIAL UNDER THE STARS

You may not realize it, but this is the time of your life! Really! Even though you are working hard and feeling the pressure to do well, this is a special time—one that will never come again. Have you ever watched people look through school yearbooks? The proof is right there in the quick smiles and nods. Sometimes they even refer to their years of schooling as "the good old days." What you may be anxious to get through now will probably become something you look back on with great nostalgia.

That's the very reason you must squeeze every ounce of goodness out of each day—and each night. If you find yourself staring up at the stars on your walk home from the game or the library, grab a few friends and dance your hearts out. It's guaranteed to turn a regular night into a night of memories.

Slow dancing isn't difficult. Just go with the flow. It's not so much about the technique as it is about the heart. And if you find yourself dancing with someone special, then the moment and the memory are just that much better.

Starlight being what it is—near-darkness—you might want to try a few new steps, risk-free. Picture yourselves in some glamorous movie, moving across the screen with grace and beauty—the new Fred Astaire and Ginger Rogers. Throw in the occasional dip, complete with dramatic flair. And don't be in a hurry. Dance until the cows come home or until curfew (whichever comes first)!

Someday you'll look back, and when you do, it's much better to say, "I'm glad I did" than "I wish I had."

5

QUIT
SKULKING
AND START
TALKING

I s there a person in one of your classes whom you've been watching? Perhaps it's someone who has impressed you with the insightful questions and clever responses she's given in class. You may have exchanged glances a few times when you were supposed to be listening to the instructor. You may even have mumbled hi as you passed in the hallway. Yet you've never had the courage to go up and introduce yourself.

Now is the time to be bold. Sure, this comes easier to some than others. Learning to put yourself out there, to initiate conversation with someone you don't know, always feels a little risky, yet it's an essential skill—one that you will need again and again after you graduate and move on to the next phase of your life. You'll be called upon to offer your hand and introduce yourself to all kinds of people in the future—professors, advisors, potential employers, clients, colleagues, strangers of all shapes and sizes, and perhaps even—watch out now!—members of the opposite sex. It won't do for you to appear shy and skittish. You will want to greet those people with a confident handshake, unwavering eye contact, and a great big smile.

What better time, what better place to work on that skill than the present, in your own familiar surroundings? So . . . go on up to that person you've been wanting to meet, offer your hand, and make a friend. It might turn out to be the only time you ever interact, but it's more likely to result in a connection that will enrich not only your life but the life of the other person as well. And while you're doing it, you'll be planting seeds of confidence and learning an important skill you'll need in the not-so-distant future and for the rest of your life.

6

WELCOME MORNINGS!

A re you the kind of person who wakes up and exclaims, "Good morning, Lord!"? Or are you the kind who wakes up muttering, "O Lord, it's morning"? You probably know exactly which category you fit into!

Mornings can be a challenge. It's easy to get into the habit of sleeping in and letting the day fall into place on the other side of 10:00 AM. Trouble is, that probably isn't working well even now while you're still in school, and it definitely won't work once you're out trying to function in the real world. Morning simply is what it is—early!

It's all in the mind-set, really. Instead of moaning at the sound of that blaring alarm clock at 6:00 AM, you can greet the morning with a prayer. "Lord, thank You for another day to live, to laugh, to learn. Thank You for the blessings that are waiting for me—blessings of friendship, understanding, love, hope, peace. And thank You for the opportunities You are going to place in my path. Awaken me, Lord, to see the world as You see it today."

The difference between a morning person and a night person is really physiological. It has to do with the way your body clock is set. It could be that you will always do your best work at night and feel challenged in the morning. That doesn't mean, however, that you can't learn to function with clarity and find enjoyment in the morning hours. If you're willing to welcome them, your mornings can become a wonderful part of your day—just as God intended.

7

HAND
OVER THE
SODA!

qua. H_2O. Water. Call it what you want as long as you drink lots of it. Most people don't drink enough water, and students are among the greatest offenders. In order to stay up for those late-night study sessions, students usually choose sugary soda or caffeinated coffee. If that's been your game plan, don't wait until after you graduate to change strategies. You'll be amazed by the difference it will make.

Consider these benefits. The first good news is that water suppresses the appetite naturally and helps the body metabolize stored fat. Simply put, water helps you lose weight. And that's just the beginning! Water carries needed nutrients throughout the body and unwanted waste out of the body, lubricates and cushions the joints, serves as a shock absorber for your eyes and spine, maintains blood volume and proper muscle tone, improves the appearance of your skin, clears your mind, and much more!

Ideally, you should drink six to eight glasses of water every day. That's a good gauge, but here's an even better one: try dividing your weight in half and drink that many ounces of water a day. That should be your goal. It's a good idea to keep a water bottle in the car, next to your computer, and anywhere else you find yourself throughout the day.

Increasing your water intake is another step toward a healthy, strong, and energetic body. In order to fulfill God's plan for your life, you'll need to be at your peak, so why not start now? On your mark, get set, *drink!*

8

NIBBLE ON SOMETHING NEW

E ver tried calamari? How about kumquats? Escargot? Ever sucked the head out of a crawfish? Well, now is the time to be daring. It's the first step to opening yourself up to new things—people, ideas, information. You are, in a sense, preparing yourself for the world outside the walls of academia.

To help you step out of your safe little food box, follow these tips to successfully scaling new culinary heights:

- ❖ Approach each new food with a positive outlook. Don't prejudge a food by texture, color, or even smell.
- ❖ Don't make yourself try a new food on its first introduction to you. If you don't want to sample calamari at tonight's dinner party, wait until next time squid is offered. It's okay.
- ❖ Don't hold a food grudge. You may have had a bad experience with a certain food at one time, and the memory of that has kept you away from it. Hey, even food deserves a second chance.
- ❖ Try a new food when you are hungry.
- ❖ Give yourself the right to dislike it. No matter how open-minded you are, some foods just won't appeal to your taste buds.
- ❖ Try only one new food at a time. Don't overwhelm yourself with too many new experiences at once.

Explore new foods now, and you'll be better able to explore bigger, more important things after you graduate. Having an open mind in one area is bound to spill over into others. Bon appétit!

9

SAVE YOUR
BREATH

S tress is just a part of life when you're a student. There are never enough minutes to complete the daily "to do" list, right? From reading hundreds of pages for an upcoming exam to writing dozens of research papers—it's a busy, intense time. You need some surefire ways to relax, stress busters that will not only help you now but also in the future. Because no matter who you are or where you go, stress is sure to follow.

While a bubble bath is always a good idea for relieving stress, it's a little difficult to bask in bubbles in the middle of a classroom. And a beach getaway is a nice stress buster, but who can just up and go to the beach on a whim? You need a practical stress buster that you can take advantage of anytime, anywhere. The answer is as close as your next breath!

- ❖ Place your left hand on your stomach and your right hand on your chest, and notice how they move with each breath.
- ❖ Now, practice filling your lungs by breathing so that your left hand goes up when you inhale, while your right hand remains still. Always inhale through your nose and exhale through your mouth. Do this eight to ten times.
- ❖ As you exhale through your mouth, make a whooshing sound as your left hand falls and then your right hand falls. Feel the tension leave your body.
- ❖ Practice breathing in and out like this for about five minutes. The movement of your abdomen and chest should be like rolling waves, rising and falling in a quiet rhythm.

While you're practicing deep breathing, think on good things and develop this attitude: "I'm too blessed to be stressed."

10

TAKE A
HOT-AIR
BALLOON
RIDE

A ah . . . a hot-air balloon ride. Does it get any better than that? There's just something magical about riding in one of those amazing crafts. If you've never boarded a balloon and headed off into the big, blue sky—now is the time!

Ask that special someone or organize a group of your best buddies and book a balloon ride. Just check the business pages of your phone book. Hot-air balloon rides are much easier to find than you might imagine. You'll want to reserve ahead—at least two or three weeks. Plan for an early morning, predawn liftoff. You will want to dress casually, but take along a sweater or jacket—breezes aloft can grow chilly.

You and your balloon mates will want to schedule plenty of time. These outings can take as much as three to four hours. The rides themselves generally last about an hour, but there's more to do to prepare for this glorious ride than turning the ignition and hitting the gas.

You probably think such an event would be out of your price range, and certainly there are cheaper forms of entertainment. Nevertheless, they are less expensive than more people think, and even if you have to save up for a year, it's one adventure that will not disappoint.

You'll relish the experience for years to come, so be sure you have a camera on board to document all the beautiful sights and the friends who shared it with you.

11

TWO WORDS— FLASHLIGHT TAG

Nothing relieves stress like a good old game of flashlight tag. You remember it, don't you? It's a combination of hide and-seek and traditional tag—played at night. You may be thinking: "Hey, I've got finals. I sure don't have time to run around chasing my friends with a flashlight." It could be that you don't have time not to run around chasing your friends with a flashlight.

You'll know when the time is right—wait for it. The words on the page of the book you're reading will start to move around until they form a picture of a farm animal. You may catch yourself thinking about eating your study notes. Or you may imagine your computer mouse crawling off into the corner and refusing to let you log on. All these are signs of a brain that's about to blow. And that's when you calmly pick up your phone and challenge five or six of your friends to a friendly game of flashlight tag. Here are the rules:

❖ The person who is It counts to a high number while everyone else hides. Then, armed with a flashlight, It searches for the other players, who will continue switching hiding places at will.

❖ When It spots someone, he or she must flash the flashlight at the individual and identify the person by name. When that happens, that person is caught and becomes It for the next round of play.

❖ To make it more interesting, have each player dress in camou-flage or dark clothing and face paint.

❖ Last, you can change it up by forming teams—guys against girls is always fun.

How you play the game isn't really important. Just make sure you play, laugh, and act as if there is nothing on earth more impor-tant than the flashlight in your hand.

12

TUTOR SOMEONE

Studying and working hard to reach your goals are good things, but they tend to keep a person pretty self-absorbed. If you're not careful, it is easy to have the attitude that everything is all about you. But something wonderful happens when you give of yourself. It changes you. It allows you to view life through a wider, more balanced lens.

"But," you say, "I don't have much to give. I don't have a lot of extra money." That may be true, but you can give of your time—and your talents. After all, not everyone is born with a head for math, or science, or English, or—maybe even basketball!

If you're paying attention, you'll probably notice someone who is struggling right away. Step up and ask that person to study with you. (You don't really have to call it "tutoring," you know.)

If you would like to be a tutor but you just aren't confident enough to approach someone your own age, you might call a local Big Brothers/Big Sisters chapter or an area boys' club or girls' club and see if there is a need for tutors in their after-school programs. Chances are, they could use some help and you're just the person to fill that void.

Another idea is to offer to help foreign students learn English as their second language. Call your area chamber of commerce and see if there is such a program in your city.

By helping someone grow in knowledge and understanding, you'll also grow in wisdom, patience, generosity, and love. All of these qualities will benefit you—no matter where you go after graduation. Tutoring someone will make you a better person. Go ahead—let the good times roll!

13

GO COSMIC BOWLING

Bowling isn't what it used to be. Forget the ugly, smelly, old bowling shoes of the past and the boring bowling games of yesteryear. Today's bowling is fashionable and fun. (Have you seen bowling shoes lately? Very cool!) Did you know that when Brad Pitt and Jennifer Aniston were together, he threw a birthday party for her at Hollywood Star Lanes? Yep, it's true! People—famous and not so famous—are discovering bowling all over again. It's totally in!

According to American Sports Data, Inc., the number of bowlers under age twenty-four increased by 26.9 million from 1997 to 2000, and the trend is continuing. Part of that increased interest is due to cosmic bowling—a combination of rock music, laser shows, and glow-in-the-dark bowling balls.

So, if you've never been cosmic bowling, you've never had cosmic fun. It's truly out of this world. Get a bunch of your buddies together and head for the nearest bowling alley. Cosmic bowling usually begins about 10:00 P.M. and goes until the wee hours of the morning. Plan on listening to everything from Maroon 5 to hip '80s music. It's not for the faint of heart. It's loud and fun and wild! And if you get tired of bowling, you can always pig out on greasy pizza, fries, and the oh-so-wonderful salty pretzels at the snack bar.

All too soon, you'll be a responsible adult, doing the things that responsible adults do—like watching TV and getting to bed early. So break away while you still can and celebrate life, freedom, and knockout bowling shoes!

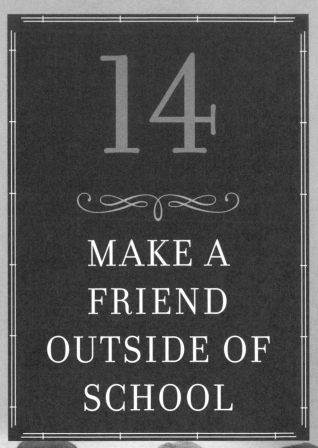

14

MAKE A FRIEND OUTSIDE OF SCHOOL

Right now you may be happy with your circle of friends—some you may have had since childhood. You study together, go to class together, share certain interests and activities—even clothes. Your friends are safe and they're fabulous. What could be gained by reaching out to someone from outside your cozy, little world?

Probably a great deal.

That person might offer a broader perspective on life than you could imagine from your rather protected place in your friendship circle. He or she might challenge your prejudices, enrich your thinking, even open your mind. In a sense, that person might be your link to the world outside—a world you will one day need to be able to navigate.

It's easy, even expected, that you have grown self-absorbed during your school years, but don't let that become a limitation. Find a friend from another school, another city, another country. Then keep the flame of friendship burning strong by corresponding, exchanging pictures, and meeting each other's friends.

You can't have too many friends, you know. That's just the way it is. Your heart and your life will expand to include the old and the new, the close by and the far away. And if you take time to nurture them, each one will bring you something wonderfully unique—something that will increase your love of life, keep you laughing, and strengthen your grasp on the world and your place in it.

15

EAT ICE CREAM FOR BREAKFAST

Do you ever feel the urge to break the rules of common sense? You know, jumping on your bed rather than making it up. Mixing the ketchup, mustard, and mayo together before you put them on your burger. If you wanted to, if you dared, you could put your darks and your lights in the same washer load— just to see what would happen.

Guess what? Everyone does stuff like that sometimes. It's completely normal. In fact, it's good for you. Eating ice cream for breakfast one day—out of the blue—won't kill you, and it might actually help you think outside the box.

The truth is that creativity is as important an attribute for success as logic, but creativity is a bit more fragile. Math and science are based on rules. Know the rules and you can always work your way to a successful outcome. But the key to creativity is the X factor. It can easily get lost.

In Scott Thorpe's book *How to Think Like Einstein*, we are told that Einstein was one of the world's most natural rule breakers. It was, in fact, the secret of his success. He knew that the greatest obstacles to creative thinking are our experiences, mistaken assumptions, half-truths, and misplaced generalities. It's good to mix it up occasionally. Watch TV while standing on your head. Put peanut butter on your pizza. Wear your T-shirt backward.

If you practice thinking like a genius before you graduate, you'll be unstoppable by the time you get your first job. Your coworkers may make some unfriendly comments about your T-shirt, but that's just because they're jealous!

16

TRY ANOTHER
HAIR COLOR—
FOR A DAY

T hey say blondes have more fun. Why not find out? Before you sit for your senior pictures or prepare for your graduation ceremony, try something new in the way of hair color. You might be surprised to discover that it can give you a whole different outlook on life.

Temporary hair color kits are easy to find—and the temporary part is quite important. Be sure you pay close attention to the directions on the box. You can find these at any drug store, discount store, even most grocery stores. The word *weekend* could also save your bacon, especially if your school has rules concerning such matters.

Another word of warning before you begin: if you have split ends, or if you already color your hair and it's a bit dry, your hair will grab color more quickly and the processing time will be less than the directions state. Always do a test strand—just to be safe.

If you're too chicken to make an extreme change, just add a few highlights or enrich your own color by a shade or two. For example, add dark red streaks to your brunette hair. Or put a black rinse on your brown hair, which will simply intensify your own color. You can always enlist the help of a friend to give you moral support as well as input, especially if your pal has experience in this area.

OK, so coloring your hair isn't a life-altering event, but it's another thing you can check off your "I was just wondering . . ." list. By the time you graduate, you should be able to cross off quite a few things. "Would pink hair work for me?" for example.

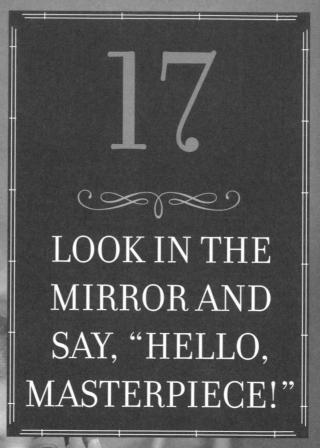

17

LOOK IN THE MIRROR AND SAY, "HELLO, MASTERPIECE!"

S ome people love looking in the mirror—but most people don't. The standards by which we judge appearance these days have become so unattainable that even the most attractive people may find themselves trying not to look too closely.

This must sadden our God who made each of us. King David put it this way in the book of Psalms:

> Oh yes, you shaped me first inside, then out;
> you formed me in my mother's womb.
> I thank you, High God—you're breathtaking!
> Body and soul, I am marvelously made!
> I worship in adoration—what a creation!
> You know me inside and out,
> you know every bone in my body;
> You know exactly how I was made, but by bit,
> how I was sculpted from nothing into something.
> Like an open book, you watched me grow from conception to birth;
> all the stages of my life were spread out before you,
> The days of my life all prepared
> before I'd even lived one day.
> (Psalm 139:13-16 MSG)

To your heavenly Father, you are a masterpiece. He doesn't care about some spread in a fashion magazine, some human conception of good looks. He sculpted you from nothing—and now you are something very special.

If you can take hold of the fact that God sees you as you are—His precious, unique creation—you will have all the self-esteem you will ever need on this side of graduation or the other. You'll be able to look into the mirror and say, "Hello, Masterpiece!"

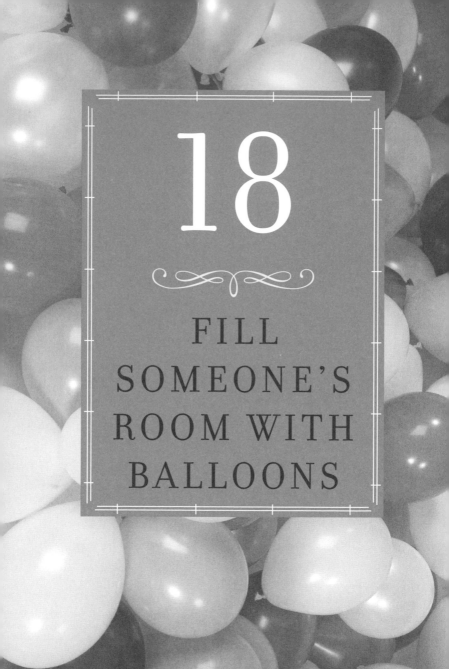

18

FILL
SOMEONE'S
ROOM WITH
BALLOONS

L ife can be mundane. But hey . . . it doesn't have to stay that way!

Find a reason to celebrate. Birthdays are handy, but just about anything will do. Say you just got a paper back in school and it wasn't a D. There you go. Why look any further?

Next you need a helium machine. (Don't panic, they're easy to find. Just check the phone book.) You'll also need lots of balloons, brightly colored ribbon, and an enthusiastic crew of workers. Once you've got that covered, select a room, absolutely any room.

Here's the plan.

Form a line for those wishing to operate the machine and keep it to five minutes per person. Don't lose track of time. These machines are great fun and some people get testy waiting for their turn. You certainly don't want to referee a fight.

With your first operator in place, begin filling the balloons. Blow them up one at a time, and pass them down the line, where the rest of the crew can tie ribbons to each one.

A few hours later, you and your crew will be amazed at the vision of delight you've created. You'll have an entire room bursting with balloon magic. Now, take hands and walk through the bodacious madness. Close your eyes and press from side to side. Balloonery is death to the mundane—squeezes it right out of the room.

Someday you may be sitting behind a desk somewhere, your head filled with corporate nonsense, when suddenly you'll close your eyes and remember when your troubles were lighter than air.

19

WRITE A MISSION STATEMENT FOR YOUR LIFE

T heodore Hesburgh, president of the University of Notre Dame from 1952 to 1987, once shared, "The very essence of leadership is that you have to have a vision. You can't blow an uncertain trumpet."

This very successful man understood the importance of having a vision and pursuing it with great passion. If you've been working so hard on completing assignments and graduating that you haven't thought about your life's vision, it's time to take your nose out of your books and write your personal mission statement.

A mission statement should address three questions:

1. What is my life about?

2. What do I stand for?

3. What action am I taking to live what my life is about and what I stand for?

Prayerfully consider each of these and make sure you communicate as specifically, yet succinctly, as possible what you wish to accomplish, who you want to be, and the character strengths and qualities you wish to cultivate through life's experiences. As with any important piece of writing, allow yourself several rough drafts before deciding on the final version.

Once you have that mission statement, post it on your bedroom mirror. Make a copy to post on your fridge. Keep a copy on the visor in your car. Put a copy in your Bible. You'll find great joy and satisfaction in setting your own path in life, knowing what you want and going after it. Refuse to settle for less!

20

❦

PLANT A
FLOWER FOR
THOSE WHO
COME LATER

Back in the old days, grads used to climb the water tower with cans of spray paint in their pockets and scrawl their name for all to see. Others carved their initials in the brick walls of school buildings. They did this to leave a permanent note for those who would come later—kind of a crude "I came, I saw, I conquered!" or "I enrolled, I passed, I graduated!" if you will.

Of course, it would be pretty tough to find a water tower these days—or even a brick wall. Such extreme measures are unnecessary anyway. There are plenty of ways to leave your mark.

One great suggestion is to do something that will enhance your school campus, like planting flowers or a flowering shrub. Please remember to ask the school administrator and groundskeeper before you try this. What a beautiful reminder this will be to those who come later that this was once your institution of learning.

And this need not be a solo endeavor. Suggest this idea to your close circle of friends, and do it together. Enlist the Latin club, your track buddies, the members of your honor society. It's something you can have a lot of fun planning and executing. It also provides a gentle, graceful, enduring reminder of the good times you've had and a signal to younger students that good times await them as well.

Flowers speak of celebration. Use them to celebrate a great period of your life and the anticipation of a terrific future. Let it be your way of saying, "I passed this way and I did it with style."

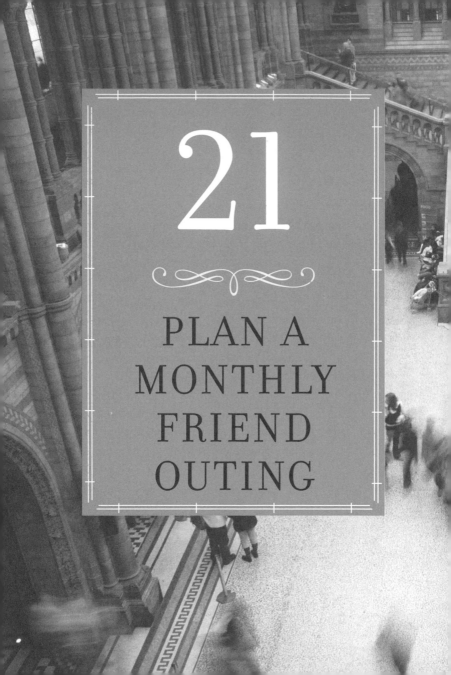

21

PLAN A
MONTHLY
FRIEND
OUTING

You know what they say—after graduation, things change, people go their separate ways. That isn't completely true. If you work at it, you can maintain school relationships for years, even for life. But it's much more difficult to remain close once you all begin to focus on what comes next.

That makes it even more important to cherish those school friendships while you have them. One way to do that is to plan a "friend outing" at least once a month. These don't have to cost a lot. We aren't talking about grand excursions. Here are a few simple ideas to get you started:

❖ Throw an all-night movie party. Rent your favorite movies, pop some popcorn, get your fluffy pillows, and plop down together for a night of food, folks, and fun.

❖ Visit a local exhibit, gallery, or museum. These activities are always more fun when you go as a group. Look for places that are off the beaten path and unique—an origami exhibit, a pottery mill, a starving artist show, a star-studded show at the planetarium, a tour of the local pie factory. You'll be surprised how many places you'll find if you're looking.

Look, laugh, talk, enjoy—you will be building memories and strengthening bonds. Let a different person choose the venue each time, and be open to widening your friend outings to include new friends. Madam, sir, your fun awaits!

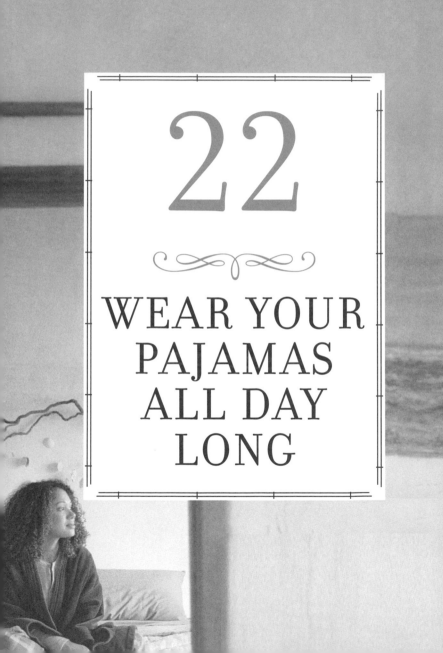

22

WEAR YOUR
PAJAMAS
ALL DAY
LONG

H ave you ever wanted to stay in your pajamas all day long? You know, forget putting on shirt, pants, shoes, or even combing your hair. You don't even have to shower if you don't want to. You do this only when you're sick? Well then, it's about time you played in your jammies all day—on purpose!

Start by picking a day   oh yes, it takes a lot of planning to pull off a day of lazy slobbery. Rule out schooldays, workdays, and church days. If that's pretty much every day, then you'll have to wait for a holiday, but it's worth the wait.

You'll need the following items:

- ❖ No fewer than four of your favorite movies
- ❖ Books (preferably novels)
- ❖ Chocolate (Note: When it comes to chocolate, "Less is more" does not apply.)
- ❖ Microwave popcorn and a suitable container
- ❖ Your favorite sodas or bottled water

If you want to be alone, put a Do Not Disturb sign on your door, turn off your phone, curl up in your favorite blanket, and hit Play. If you get hungry, simply call out for pizza.

But what if you are one of those people who prefer not to lounge alone? In that case, invite a friend or two to join you. Make sure you give them plenty of time to plan as well. Not only will you have a day to remember long after graduation, but you will find some rest for your weary soul as well.

23

~~~

GIVE IT UP
FOR THE
HOME TEAM

N ever again in life are your loyalties likely to be so clear-cut as when you're sitting in the stands cheering away for your home team. No ambiguities to deal with. No one is asking you to choose between ABC, NBC, CBS, or FOX. You don't have to struggle with deciding if you are a Republican or a Democrat. You aren't being asked to choose one corporate product over another. No value judgments to make. This is one time when you're simply for the home team—no ifs, ands, or buts about it.

In this wonderful, unconflicted world, yell like a banshee and have a really great time. Shout until you can hear your voice getting tired. And when you're not shouting, whistle and wave. Relax and let your worries fly as well. Sure, it's just a game. But games serve a purpose. They give us permission to play. And playing allows us to let off steam, rest our brains, and ignore our inhibitions.

And by the way, you don't even have to like sports to join in with this kind of fun. Just follow the cheerleaders and listen to those around you. You don't have to know a home run from a touchdown to enter in and have a great time. Even if the home team loses, chances are you'll go home feeling like a winner.

You will have plenty of time after graduation to take a stand on important, controversial issues. For now, enjoy the fact that you can enjoy going along with the crowd.

24

PICTURES,
PICTURES,
PICTURES!

THINGS YOU SHOULD DO BEFORE YOU GRADUATE

Pictures tell the stories of our lives and keep friends and family close at hand. Now, sooner, later—it's always a good idea to take lots and lots of pictures. One of your friends has a new haircut or hair color, a new dog, new wheels, a new swimsuit, new skis, a new bedspread. No doubt about it, each "new" requires a new picture. And that's just the beginning! Your school life must be documented, and you can't depend on the yearbook staff to do it all. You must take matters into your own hands!

If you don't have a good camera, don't sweat it. Just buy a disposable one and keep it with you for impromptu photo sessions. Or you might purchase several so you can keep one in your backpack, one in the glove compartment of your car (as long as it's not too hot), and one in your room. If you have a camera phone, you're just that much more prepared.

Here are a few tips that will ensure that you get great photos you'll appreciate long after graduation.

- ❖ Having people pose is fine, but try taking candid shots of friends and fellow classmates in their natural surroundings.
- ❖ Make sure the sun isn't behind the subjects of your photos or shining directly into their eyes, causing them to squint.
- ❖ Take horizontal and vertical pictures in order to get a variety of shots.

After you've taken tons of pictures, why not put together special scrapbooks for your best buddies? Photo albums/scrapbooks make treasured gifts that last a lifetime. Okay then—ready, set, snap!

25

CONDUCT A
CLOTHING
INVENTORY

If you're like most students, your closet is full of jeans, jeans, and more jeans . . . with a few sweatshirts and dozens of T-shirts thrown in for good measure. While these are perfectly good outfits for going to class and hanging out with your friends on weekends, they aren't exactly ideal for some of the activities you will want to take part in after graduation. Waiting until you need nice outfits is the expensive, stressful way to go about it. It's so much more fun to assess your situation and spruce up your closet over time.

Here are six quick tips to help you get started:

- ❖ Study fashion magazines, earmarking the pages that contain your favorite looks.
- ❖ Go to a department store and try on various styles of suits, dress pants, sweaters, jackets, and dress shoes, and determine which styles are most flattering.
- ❖ Start budgeting enough money to purchase one or two key pieces each month.
- ❖ Buy basic items that will mix and match well so that you can maximize the number of outfits in your wardrobe.
- ❖ Choose a traditional style of clothing as opposed to a trendy one that will go out of fashion more quickly.
- ❖ Update some of the clothes you already own by purchasing new accessories.

A quality wardrobe is an investment in your future. Whether you're interviewing for a scholarship, internship, or your first splash into the professional world, having the right clothes will give you confidence and help you look like the winner you already are.

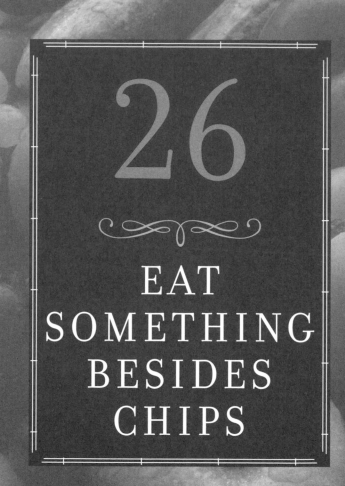

26

EAT
SOMETHING
BESIDES
CHIPS

Y ou're a student, and students are time-challenged. It's tough to think through and adopt healthy eating habits when you're flying through your classes, holding down a part-time job, playing sports, writing papers, studying for exams. It's easier to grab something on the run. But you can still make good choices and now is the time to make them. The sooner the better.

Here are a few fast-food facts to put you on the road to healthier eating:

- ❖ A plain hamburger has only 280 calories and 10 grams of fat, while a Big Mac or its equivalent from another vendor is about 590 calories and 34 grams of fat. Add a large order of fries and you're chowing down more than 1,000 calories and almost 60 grams of fat. We won't even think about the sugary soft drink that finishes out the combo.
- ❖ A grilled chicken Caesar salad has only 100 calories and 2.5 grams of fat (and fat-free herb vinaigrette dressing has only 35 calories). On the other hand, a nine-piece order of chicken nuggets comes to about 430 calories and 25 grams of fat. Dipping sauces add another 40 to 60 calories.

You may not be willing to settle for a plain hamburger and none of the yummy sides, but at least you can start thinking about what you eat and making gradual improvements, even while you're pulling into the drive through.

Ask for a nutritional menu at each of your favorite fast-food restaurants or go online to learn the facts. Knowledge is power—the power to make informed choices that will serve you before you graduate and after.

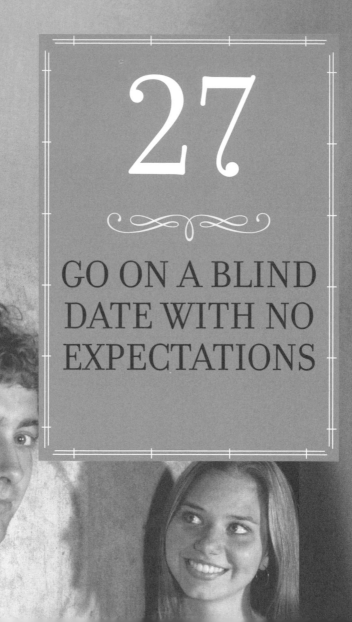

27

GO ON A BLIND
DATE WITH NO
EXPECTATIONS

Blind dates: even if you're a pretty secure single, that phrase can send a shiver dancing up your spine. Perhaps that's because too often these dates are full of unrealistic, even ridiculous, expectations.

But with the right attitudes, a blind date could be a great deal of fun, an adventure even. When the pressure to find romance is removed, this much-feared activity simply becomes an opportunity to meet someone new.

Here are some blind-date tips to help you have a great time without all the pressure:

- ❖ Make it a group date with well-known friends along for the ride.
- ❖ Don't take yourself or the date too seriously.
- ❖ Avoid superficial impressions.
- ❖ Have a backup plan. (Someone who will help you if you begin to feel uncomfortable.)
- ❖ Always meet in a public place.
- ❖ Choose an activity that has a beginning and an end—such as bowling two games, for example.
- ❖ Balance talking and listening. Don't be a bore and talk endlessly about yourself. Make sure you ask open-ended questions and listen intently to the answers.

The occasional blind date can teach you to think on your feet and hone your social skills. Your future will entail meeting, working, and socializing with people you don't know. When that happens you want to be able to reach out with confidence, unperturbed. These are skills better learned sooner than later and blind dates are a great way to have fun while you practice.

28

TAKE COMMAND
OF THE STAGE—
EVEN IF IT'S
JUST TO MOVE
SCENERY

T o be or not to be . . . that is the question."

Or maybe it's actually the answer. Getting involved in your school's theatrical productions is a great way to meet new people and become part of something quite magical. Maybe you're not the next Kevin Spacey or an aspiring Nicole Kidman, but you can make a valuable contribution by helping with the lighting, costumes, sets, stage direction, or moving the scenery between acts.

In addition to meeting new people, you'll also have the opportunity to overcome stage fright if you take on a speaking part. By learning to face your fears head-on, you'll become more effective when you're called upon to speak before a group in the future. And let's face it; public speaking is part of most every career these days. So why not get a jump-start on your professional skills now, so after graduation you'll be better prepared to make presentations with confidence and finesse?

Getting involved in the theater is also a healthy way to escape "the real world" for a few hours each week. Whether you're lost in the lovely language of Shakespeare or singing your heart out in *The Music Man*, the theater is a great, inexpensive, and totally intoxicating activity.

Playwright Arthur Miller once said, "The theater is so endlessly fascinating because it's so accidental. It's so much like life." If that's true, then participating in the theater is great preparation for what is to come. Go ahead and get involved. The stage is calling you . . . don't you hear it?

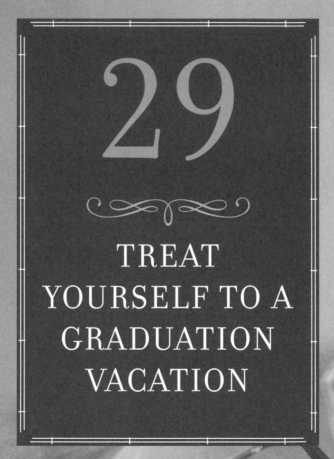

29

TREAT YOURSELF TO A GRADUATION VACATION

S weet vacation! You've earned some time off. Now's the time to plan a great trip—something really special—to celebrate once you have that coveted diploma in hand.

Travel consultants say you need to know what kind of vacationer you are before planning that perfect graduation getaway, however. Here are some guidelines that might help you determine what kind of vacation best suits your personality.

You might be a beach bum if . . .

- ❖ you love to swim.
- ❖ you long to work on your tan.
- ❖ you are more of a laid-back person.

You might be an adventurer if . . .

- ❖ you need to participate in activity to be happy.
- ❖ you are very physically fit.
- ❖ you are constantly on the lookout for an adventure.

You might be a sightseer if . . .

- ❖ you want to learn while vacationing.
- ❖ you are interested in history or art.

Once you've identified which type of vacationer you are, follow these steps:

1. Decide where you want to go and how much activity you want to engage in when you're there.
2. If you have a travel consultant, contact that expert for assistance in making the best choice for your vacation.
3. Go to the library or use the Internet to find out information about the destination of your choice.
4. Determine how much money you can invest in this venture.

Research it. Plan it. Book it. And enjoy it! Think of this trip as a reward for your hard work. You deserve it!

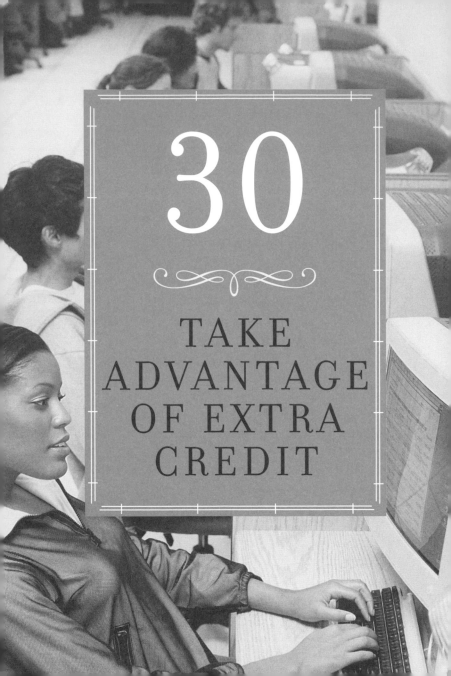

30

TAKE
ADVANTAGE
OF EXTRA
CREDIT

Every honor student knows a little secret: "extra credit" is much more than some teacher's idea of a sick joke. You've just completed an excruciating essay entitled "Beowolf: Middle English for the Masses," you've had six hours of sleep in the last two nights, and you can barely stay awake to turn it in. Then the teacher says—out of the blue—that she will add ten extra points to your final grade if you will take a few minutes to cite which three resources from the school library best helped you complete your paper. Your head is screaming, "Is she kidding me? Resources? Library? Forgetaboutit!"

But you'd be amazed what those few extra points can do. Off your game for an important exam? A day or two late with a big paper? Extra credit is the great equalizer. It can literally move your grade from a C to a B, from a B to an A. If you can reach down deep inside and find the strength to tackle it, extra credit is the equivalent of an academic savings account that no serious student can afford to ignore.

Most opportunities for extra credit are spelled out in your syllabus or by the teacher early in the term. There's no excuse for missing out on that. But it's also a good idea to keep your ears open for unexpected opportunities that might come up as the class progresses—these are gold for the diligent prospector.

It would be a shame to wait until graduation to realize that you could have done better. Life is about opportunities taken. Take advantage of all those that come your way, no matter how small.

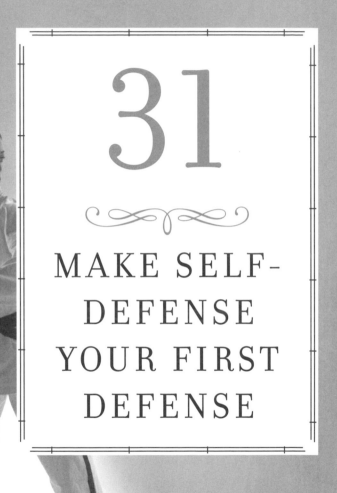

31

MAKE SELF-DEFENSE YOUR FIRST DEFENSE

S orry to say it, but we live in a dangerous world. Learning how to defend yourself and stay safe is more than a good idea, it's an absolute necessity. Fortunately, this is one activity that offers more than solid information—it's really great exercise and a lot of fun.

Call the YMCA and inquire about self-defense classes offered in any of its local facilities. Or check local gyms for classes in tae kwon do, karate, etc. You'll find yourself more aware of your surroundings and brimming with confidence after just a few sessions.

If the thought of attending such a class by yourself leaves you feeling a little apprehensive, get a couple of friends to go with you. You'll be surprised how many laughs you'll have just learning how to set your feet and move your arms properly. And in the end, you'll know something that you did not know before: how to ward off an attacker.

You may not ever have to use it. When the thugs see your confident stride, odds are they won't even try. Such cowards are looking for easy prey rather than someone who is apt to give them a fight.

It's never too early to learn to take care of yourself. It's something you'll have in your personal arsenal during every phase of your life. Do it for yourself. Do it for those who love you.

And if you're a guy who's thinking this suggestion is just for girls—think again. Get out there and get safe!

32

SHUN
PROCRASTINATION!

By definition, procrastination is the habit of putting tasks off to the last possible minute. Why do we do that to ourselves? Who knows—but we do, and our failure to move forward causes missed opportunities, long and frenzied work hours, stress, and feelings of resentment, guilt, and being overwhelmed. Who wants to deal with all that unpleasantness? You've got better things to do!

Here are three ways to combat procrastination:

1. Replace "Finish it" with "Begin it." Do your task in small increments. Beginning the task is half the battle.
2. Focus on the now instead of the future. Don't borrow tomorrow's trouble today. Focus on the task at hand—not the "to do" list for next week.
3. Replace perfectionism with good work. If you think you have to do everything perfectly, you might become too overwhelmed to ever begin. Give yourself the luxury of being human.

Don't delay your dreams with procrastination—get going! You have a big, full, spectacular life ahead of you, and now is the time to begin living it to the fullest. Start small, tackling one thing at a time, and before you know it, you'll be replacing a habit of procrastination with the habit of being proactive. That's a swing from failure to fabulous!

33

TRAVEL LIGHT

You'll pick up many important skills while you're working on educating yourself, like time and money management, social interaction, and writing for a variety of purposes. But one skill will benefit you for a lifetime no matter where your destiny calls you after graduation. Whether you are sitting on the beach at Key West or riding an elephant in Thailand, your trip will be more enjoyable and less stressful if you know how to pack for the road.

The following are simple guidelines to help you on your way:

- ❖ Don't try to take everything you own. If you overfill a suitcase, your clothing will get crushed and the other contents may be damaged. Take out what you don't need—a second jacket, too many pairs of shoes—and if necessary, pack another bag.
- ❖ Don't under-fill your suitcase either, because the contents can shift during travel. This could result in wrinkling your clothing and damaging your toiletries.
- ❖ Lay out everything you plan to pack, making sure you include all the pieces to each ensemble. Then, rather than packing randomly, start by putting the heavier items, like shoes, on the bottom.
- ❖ Roll items like socks and underwear and put them in the empty spaces.
- ❖ For a big trip, use special vacuum-storage bags. These bags will decrease the size of each item, and clothing will emerge from the bags wrinkle-free.
- ❖ Put every liquid in its own self-sealing plastic bag.

Packing isn't brain surgery, but it's important. It can mean the difference between a good trip and a great one!

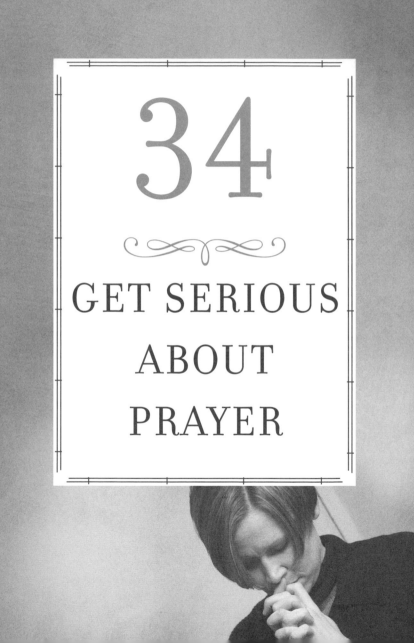

34

GET SERIOUS
ABOUT
PRAYER

Many people look at prayer as a task to be accomplished. That way of thinking simply takes the fun out of it. Prayer really is about communicating. In fact, it's about conversing—talking and listening, listening and talking—with God.

Think of it this way: you're with your friends all day, talking and hanging out, and then you part and go your separate ways. That's when you hook up by cell phone. Then when you get home, you exchange e-mail messages. Friends are like that. They can't get enough time together. They want to talk over everything at length. Even simple details of life warrant a connection.

That's exactly how God intended prayer to be: an open conversation with no real beginning and no end. He wants to be in our hearts and on our minds, always in contact wherever we go. That doesn't mean you can't set aside some quality time for a nice long heart-to-heart, but that would be your choice, your privilege, your special time with the best Friend of all.

Prayer is the single most important habit you can take with you as you head into the next phase of your life. Go ahead and leave behind the trappings of prayer: the mandated time on your knees, the obligatory prayer when you awaken and before you go to sleep at night. Start talking to God as one person to another, getting to know Him as a Friend. Soon you'll find that the real conversation has begun. And though there will be times of silence between you, you'll learn that even those times make your endless conversation richer, deeper, and more satisfying.

35

❦

EMBRACE
DIVERSITY

T he world is a big place, but it's becoming smaller every day. New technologies have literally erased the obstacles of time and space in a way that allows us to see and feel the pain of those who live all over the globe. We watched the tsunami crash ashore in Thailand, the flood waters engulf New Orleans, the earthquake's aftermath in Pakistan. No longer can we be a people unto ourselves—blissfully unaware of global heartache and need.

In addition to allowing us to view the tragedy of distant people and places, technology makes it possible to better understand their cultures and customs. We have become a world energized by diversity. The abilities and understanding once reserved for missionaries and service providers who work abroad are now needed to succeed in any arena. The sooner you are able to nurture a positive world view, to embrace diversity, the better you will be able to function even here in these United States.

You probably already have friends from other nationalities and cultures. If so, take time to ask questions and get to know more about how they do things. Expose yourself to new ways of thinking and alternative mind-sets. You'll find such conversations both enlightening and fun.

Living in a global neighborhood means tearing down walls and opening up lines of communication. Why wait for someone else to take the lead? The first ones at the party get the best seats!

36

❦

READ YOUR BIBLE COVER TO COVER

No matter where you go in life, your Bible needs to go with you. It's the ultimate road map for your journey. Some call it an "owner's manual." No matter what you call it, it contains the words of life. Within its pages lie much wisdom, knowledge, understanding, and insight. Psalm 119:105 says it is a lamp to our feet and a light for our path.

The Bible also contains all of the promises that belong to you as a child of God. You need to know what those promises are so that you can grab hold of them and rely on them through good times and bad.

As you read through your Bible, you'll also find "The Big Ten" and other such commandments that God has given to keep us from getting entangled in difficult and painful situations. Did you think God put them there just so He'd have a good reason to scold you? No. All His actions toward us are those of a loving Father. Your parents had the same kind of rules when you were growing up: "Don't play in the street. Don't speak to strangers. Don't swim alone." They were all intended to keep you safe, and God gave His commandments with the same intention.

The Bible is the most important book you will ever read. Why wait? Get started now before you graduate. Dig in, take notes, use your highlighter. Start at the beginning and don't stop until you've read every page. The benefits will begin to stack up immediately, but they will continue for a lifetime.

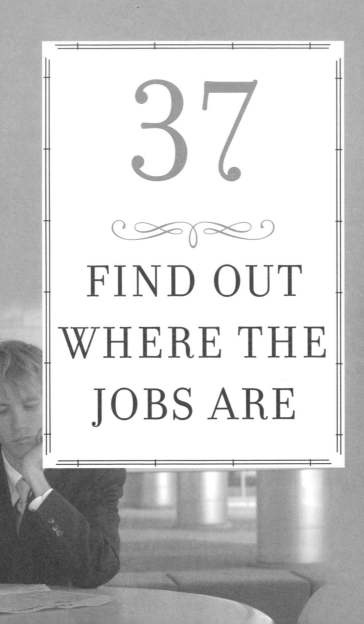

37

FIND OUT
WHERE THE
JOBS ARE

No matter where you are in your education, it's never too soon to begin checking out the job market. Start scanning the local classifieds for openings in your chosen career field. Check online classified ads for interesting job opportunities in every part of the world. View this activity as productive fun.

Make this a time for dreaming as well as for research. Look into jobs you never thought you could actually do—be an elephant trainer or magazine model, for example—and check them out just for fun. You might have a surprise in store.

You would also benefit from attending a career fair in your area. Don't limit yourself to picking up literature only in your chosen field. Have an open mind. Maybe you've never considered a career in public relations, for example. What would it hurt to stop by and speak to a company's representatives? If nothing else, you'll learn something new and narrow your job search by eliminating PR work as a possible future option. Either way, you'll leave more enriched and your time won't be wasted.

Researching the job market is a great way to help you identify your true calling—that occupation that fits you like a glove and provides a lifetime of satisfaction.

38

DEVELOP
YOUR GIFTS
AND TALENTS

J esus told his disciples a story that goes like this: A nobleman prepares for a journey by entrusting his property to his servants. To the first he gives five talents (a certain weight of silver), to the next two talents, and to the last he gives one talent. Then he leaves on his journey. When he returns, he learns that the servant to whom he had given five talents doubled the amount through wise investments. The second servant also gave the master twice as much as he had received. Both were praised!

But the third servant—the one who had been given one talent—had simply buried his silver in the ground. Though he returned it intact, the master was displeased. The servant had made no effort to invest what the master had entrusted to him.

You may be saying, "No one has given me any silver to invest, at least not that I remember!" But this parable is about much more than silver. It's about making good investments with what God has given you. And on a very personal level, that includes your personal abilities.

There are many ways to invest your nonmonetary talents, but whatever you do, don't bury them deep within yourself and leave them untended. The day will come when your Creator will ask for an accounting. What will you have to offer? A voice trained and poised to sing His praises? Skilled writing that brings glory to His name? An artistic masterpiece, the result of years of practice? Your talent may be small and hardly noticeable or grand and constantly on display. You may have five gifts or just one. That part doesn't matter. Be sure that you have prudently invested what God has entrusted to you.

39

SUBSCRIBE
TO A
PROFESSIONAL
MAGAZINE

Of course, we all love to read the gossip rags and the occasional sports magazine, but what about reading a publication that could actually benefit you in your future endeavors? That's what a professional magazine can do for you.

Begin by going to your local library and checking out the publications in the fields you think you might want to pursue. Inside you will find the nitty-gritty of each profession—the good, the bad, and sometimes even the ugly. You'll read articles by those who are actually doing the work. You'll familiarize yourself with insider terms and read about real day-to-day challenges people are facing. You will learn about new technology and find out who the movers and shakers are. You may discover that there are certain tools you'll need for your profession, what they are, and how much it might cost to purchase them.

Let's say you would like to be a veterinarian. In the sundry professional publications for vets, you can find out new scholastic requirements for the field, what areas of the country offer the most jobs, what type of individual does best in this field, and much more.

Continue to sponge off the library—that's what it's there for—until you have a specific idea of what you'd like to do. Once you've committed to a certain field, go ahead and subscribe. It's money well spent preparing you for all the great things that are to come.

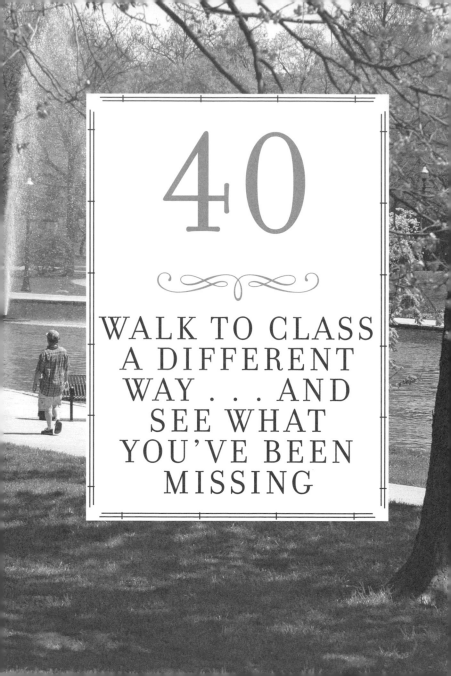

40

WALK TO CLASS
A DIFFERENT
WAY . . . AND
SEE WHAT
YOU'VE BEEN
MISSING

We tend to be creatures of habit. We sit in the same seat at church every Sunday. We order the same foods at our favorite restaurants. We visit the same theater. We walk to class the same way every day. Perhaps it is because there is security in the familiar, but oftentimes we get into a rut and take things for granted. So why not change it up a bit? Start by walking to class a different way this week. Take the time to explore and purposely take in your surroundings.

If you are now asking, "What's the big deal? I get there, don't I?" then consider these possible benefits. Perhaps you'll meet someone new or see something you didn't know existed. Maybe it will open up a new neuro-pathway in your brain. Hey . . . really!

You see, the trouble with doing things the same way every time is that studies tell us it actually leaves a crease or a rut in your gray matter over time. That's why we form habits. Once that pathway is established, it's actually possible to tune out your surroundings so that you barely notice them. You focus on getting to class on time and the rest just fades into the outskirts of your consciousness.

Of course, urging you to walk a different way to class is actually just a tag for encouraging you to change it up a little in all those little things you do habitually. Hold your toothbrush with your other hand for a while or eat something different for breakfast. These little changes will awaken your senses and keep those brain cells moving.

41

LISTEN TO
THE VOICE OF
EXPERIENCE

A very wise person once said, "Experience is the worst teacher; it gives the test before presenting the lesson." That's the truth, isn't it? Think back on your life so far. If you knew then what you know now, wouldn't you have made some different (possibly better) decisions? We all would have.

The way to take the edge off that reality is to appreciate the fact that there are many people who have far more experience than you have, people who have suffered calamities and learned important lessons from them. They have walked down certain paths and know what to expect at the far end. These individuals know where to find the buried treasure and how to stay out of the quicksand pit on their way to digging it up. Who are these savvy individuals? Well . . .

Many of them go by Grandpa and Grandma. Others are parents, sisters, brothers, uncles, aunts, teachers, friends, counselors, doctors, pastors, etc. You rub shoulders with the voices of experience every day.

Talk to your grandparents. Ask their advice about big life issues. Talk to your parents—yes, they do know more than you do. Learn from those in your chosen field who've been doing what you dream of doing. Run your ideas and questions by them. Ask if they'd be willing to mentor you as you embark on the path they've already traveled. Most importantly, ask God. He's been around longer than anyone and He knows everything!

The Bible says that those who seek wisdom shall find it, so seek diligently! Embrace the voice of experience. This next phase of life will require all the wisdom you can muster.

42

CREATE
A BASIC
BUDGET

Budget: there—it's been said and no one actually got hurt. This much-maligned concept is most unpopular, but it can really be a person's best friend. Try to take hold of the following truth: budgets increase your spending power rather than taking it away.

It's sad to think that many people don't know how much money they have or how to make it work for them. They simply spend until it's gone and then suffer until they get more. That's not a very comfortable way to live. The answer is to plan out your spending and match it to your income, so that you don't ever have to do without.

It's pretty simple really. You can do the math. Figure out what it costs to live each month—you know, the bills you have to pay on a regular basis. Now, add up your income, anything that comes to you from a job, your parents, or any other source. If the difference is on the plus side, you can look at those as your discretionary funds. You can put some of them away for emergencies, save for a big purchase, or fritter them away on odds and ends. That's your call.

If the difference between your expenses and your income is on the minus side, you will need to make some adjustments. Perhaps you can add some hours at work, drive your car less, eliminate some of your monthly charges. And honestly, the whole process takes only a few minutes—thirty at the most.

Setting a budget and living by it establish a good precedent in your life so that as your income increases (and it will!), you'll be able to fully enjoy the rewards of your efforts.

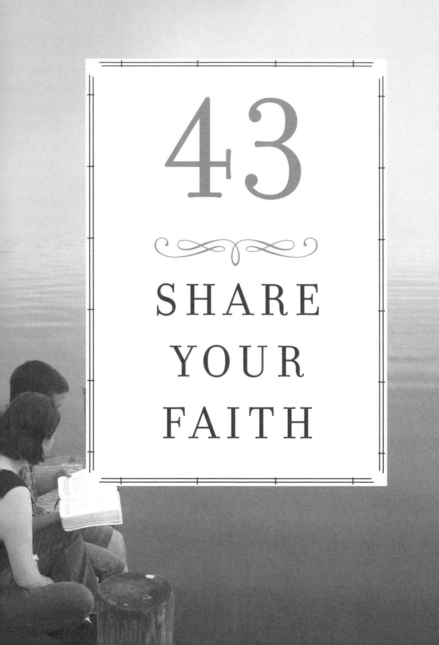

43

SHARE
YOUR
FAITH

You don't have to sport "witness wear" in order to share your faith. You don't even have to have a "Honk if you love Jesus" bumper sticker on the back of your car. You don't have to stand on the corner passing out flyers or wear a sign that says, "Jesus Saves." You simply have to live your faith in front of others, letting Jesus shine on the inside of you and allowing His love to flow through you. God will take care of the rest.

Ask God to help you listen to the conversations going on around you, give you a sensitivity to those who are hurting, make you the kind of person who is approachable with questions. That's the way Jesus did it—and it worked!

All people really want is to know the truth. They don't want it crammed down their throats. They need it in smaller, more digestible portions. They want to be able to judge its credibility. There are so many other things competing for their attention. But as they get to know you, as they see that your words and actions are in harmony, they will be drawn to you and your faith. Jesus fed His followers bread for their bodies and bread for their souls. He couched His words in parables and stories. He proved His statements by backing them up with miracles. He expects only that you follow His lead.

Share your stories (how God has changed your life), state your beliefs (simply and honestly, when asked), and give people time to digest what you've said. When you do these things, the Holy Spirit will come along to endorse your words by moving on people's hearts and drawing them to Him.

44

❦

EMBRACE
SELF-
RULE!

Being a child is a lot of fun. While adults labor away at jobs and take care of the business of living, kids get to play the days away. No matter what happens, someone older, someone wiser picks up the slack. The problem is that some people never want to leave the warmth and security of a dependent lifestyle. They may pay it lip service, but the truth is they like not having to be responsible for their choices or suffer the consequences of their mistakes. If someone else makes all their decisions, someone else is held responsible. Many people—men and women alike—live like grown-up kids their whole lives.

In a way, it's kind of understandable. Ruling yourself is hard work. It takes time and effort and determination to take care of that big paper, study for that important exam, show up at work on time every day without someone standing over you making you do it. It's not easy to grow up, no matter what age you may be.

The thing is, though, that until you can rule yourself, your life won't amount to much. You will never be able to leave your distinctive mark on the world. You won't be able to accomplish the plan for which you were created.

Begin to self-rule by making one important decision at a time and carrying through. Each one will encourage you to make the next, and the next, and the next. Embrace the experience, no matter how difficult, as your rite of passage into the adult world. Celebrate each accomplishment, each victory, with a big, inner pat on the shoulder.

The more you learn to responsibly rule yourself now, the more successful and accomplished you will be later.

45

TRY EVERY
FLAVOR OF
JELLY BEANS—
AND SHARE!

I t seems as if jelly beans have been around forever. Do a little survey and you'll probably find out that even the oldest people you know remember eating them as children. Former President Reagan (remember him?) said, "You can tell a lot about a man by his way of eating jelly beans." He was known to serve them at cabinet meetings, and tradition has it that blueberry jelly beans, produced by Jelly Bellies, were created just so he could serve red, white, and blue beans at his 1981 inauguration. President Reagan did for jelly beans what President Washington did for cherry trees.

And yes, there is a point to all this!

Like many other colorful, bite-sized, relatively inexpensive candies, jelly beans are fun and just right for sharing. When you're dragging, at the end of a long term, a jelly bean break can really pick you up and set you on the other side of the doldrums.

They can be counted, separated by color, taste tested for accuracy of flavor. They provide the mindless activity and conversation that you need to escape the tyranny of the endless stream of papers and tests and course requirements. They provide an opportunity to stop for a moment and have fun with friends.

This probably isn't the most important lesson you should learn before you graduate, but it does have merit. Jelly beans, like many other things, are stress busters. Stress can weaken your body and ravage your mind and emotions, and it's a constant in the Western world. Just remember that something as simple as a jelly bean can help to take the edge off.

46

PREPARE TO
CELEBRATE

I n the midst of fulfilling all of your academic requirements and planning for a prosperous future, celebrating all of your hard work shouldn't be pushed to the back burner. No, now is the time to celebrate! Of course, the big celebration will come once you move that tassel on your cap from one side to the other, but there's no harm in getting a jump on the festivities! Each week until graduation, reward yourself in some small way.

For example, if you've been working out and eating healthy foods, go ahead and splurge on a hot fudge sundae with your best friend. If you've been wisely budgeting and saving for future possibilities, buy yourself a new outfit or a new pair of shoes that will take you into your future with added confidence. If you've been longing to attend a concert or a Broadway show, make plans to do so. Get online and order those tickets, and give yourself something to look forward to—something you've really dreamed of doing.

Celebrating only the big accomplishments will leave you with far too few celebrations in your life. Life itself should be celebrated daily. Celebrate the rising and setting of the sun. Remember, that particular skyscape will never happen again. Celebrate your friends, especially those you won't see much of after graduation. And celebrate the fact that God loves you and has a wonderful plan for you, something so marvelous that you can't even imagine it now.

You have a lot to celebrate. You'd better get started right away.

47

~~~~~~

LEARN THE
BASICS—OF
COOKING

E ven if cooking is not your bag and you have no aspirations of becoming a gourmet chef, you still ought to know your way around a kitchen. Let's face it: going out to eat all the time can really blow your budget, and visiting the fast-food drive-through on a regular basis can bulk up your waistline. So learning to cook is a must.

But if you really don't like to cook or you don't have time to spend poring through recipes that have twenty-five ingredients or more, you'll need to purchase a basic cookbook. Here's a good one to start with: *How to Cook Everything: Simple Recipes for Great Food* by Mark Bittman. This 960 page book covers everything from real buttered popcorn to black bean soup. From appetizers to dessert, this book has it all. It is divided into twenty-three sections, covering cooking equipment, technique, easy tips, and recipes. New, it costs about twenty-two dollars on *www.Amazon.com* but you can get a used version for around ten dollars. If that's a bit big for your tastes, try *Betty Crocker's Cooking Basics: Learning to Cook with Confidence,* or *Help! My Apartment Has a Kitchen Cookbook: 100+ Great Recipes with Foolproof Instructions.* You can find those on Amazon too.

Once you've got a cookbook that works for you, the rest is just a matter of learning as you go. Practice whenever you have an opportunity and after graduation, you'll be—drum roll, please—able to feed yourself!

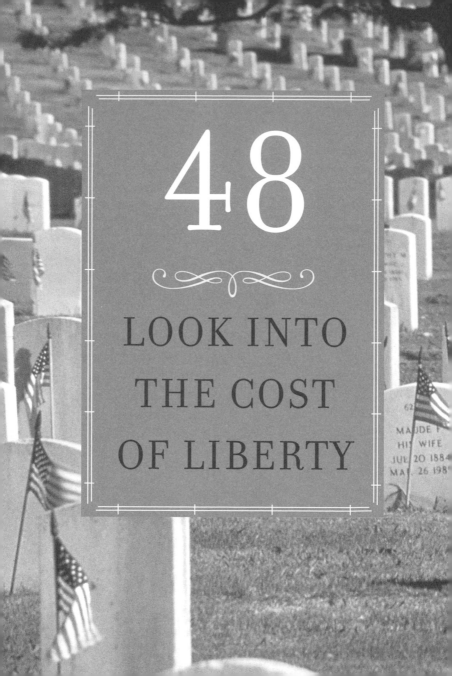

48

LOOK INTO
THE COST
OF LIBERTY

Thomas Jefferson once said, "I would rather be exposed to the inconveniences attending too much liberty than those attending too small a degree of it."

No doubt about it: liberty is important to every society. Patrick Henry valued it so much that he stated, "Give me liberty, or give me death"—one of the most familiar declarations in American history.

So accustomed are we to our freedoms, however, that it's easy to take them for granted. That must not happen, for every generation must do its part if liberty is to continue to burn brightly in our nation.

Liberty comes at a high price. Literally millions of men and women have given their lives in defense of it. Your future life in the world at large, your success in your profession, your ability to make personal choices that affect yourself and your loved ones, your license to speak your mind, and your freedom to worship when, where, and how you choose—all these things were bought with the blood, sweat, tears, families, and fortunes of those who were willing to lay down everything, even their lives, for this country.

Do something positive to express your gratitude. Send a letter of thanks to a veteran; attend a Veterans' Day celebration; when you see someone in uniform, stop and offer a word of thanks for his or her service; pray for those who labor in war zones around the world. The best way to secure your liberty is to be grateful for it—actively, assertively grateful.

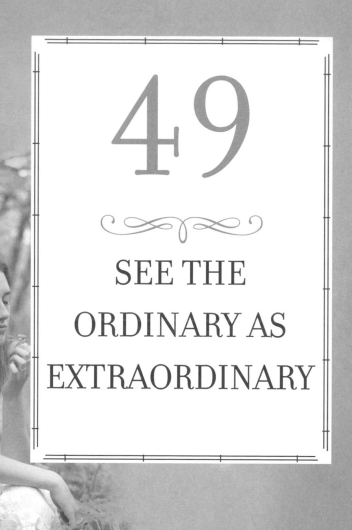

49

SEE THE ORDINARY AS EXTRAORDINARY

F or some people, each day is filled with excitement and discovery. Do you know someone like that? Those individuals have been blessed with a truly special gift. They have the ability to see the extraordinary in the ordinary situations and encounters of everyday life.

Even though some people are born with this ability already in place, all of us can learn to practice the powerful principle it represents. Look around you. Focus on someone you've known for a long time, someone completely familiar. Now, really look. What do you see? Just regular old Susan or Duke or Ethan? Or do you see a truly unique individual, more delicately distinctive even than a snowflake? Have you ever really stopped to listen to the timbre of that person's voice, noticed the tilt of the head, the color of the eyes? God is an awesome Creator who never creates anyone or anything the same way twice. That means your comfortable, familiar friend is anything but "regular."

Now take a look at the colors of your world. Each green, each yellow, each red, each blue is different and special. Each wood has its own look and feel, each flower its distinctive leaf and bud.

This is a great skill to develop as you anticipate leaving school and entering the next phase of your life, whether it's more school or the job market. It will enhance your view of the world around you, make you a better judge of character, spur your creativity, feed your passion for life, and fill your days with good things, the ordinary things that are really so much more.

50

PRACTICE
RANDOM
ACTS OF
KINDNESS

Someone once said, "It's difficult to give away kindness. It keeps coming back to you." Did you know that kindness is an action word? Just ask the folks who established The Random Acts of Kindness Foundation in 1995. Its sole mission is to inspire people to practice kindness.

It's a great concept, isn't it? Join in on the fun and look for ways to pass on kindness today. By getting in the habit of doing good deeds before you graduate, you'll be establishing a worthy pattern for the rest of your life. Kindness never goes out of style and there will never be enough of it. A person is wise to cultivate it as an active part of his or her routine.

Here are some ideas to help you get started:

1. Give away something to someone who needs it more.
2. Collect goods for a food bank.
3. Visit a stranger in a nursing home.
4. Help someone who has nothing to offer in return.
5. Pay the toll for the person behind you.
6. Become generous with sincere compliments.
7. Take time to pray for others.
8. Say something nice whenever you can.
9. Give the gift of a smile.

Even simple things can make an impact when they are done without self-interest. And the most surprising thing: as you sow seeds of kindness, you'll be the one who benefits most, for it is truly more blessed to give than receive. It's one of the guiding principles of God's world.

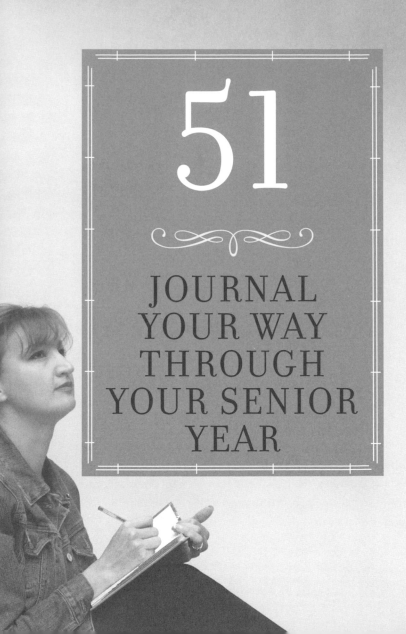

51

JOURNAL
YOUR WAY
THROUGH
YOUR SENIOR
YEAR

N ot everyone enjoys journaling; in fact, some people really dislike any writing exercise. Yet journaling can be a very beneficial activity. Perhaps you get writer's cramp because your hand can't keep up with the speed of your thoughts. If that's the case, try typing on your computer. You might even want to consider blogging—keeping a Weblog—on the Internet. This avenue for recording one's thoughts has become increasingly popular. (A word of caution, however: if you do choose to blog, you might want to conceal your identity for safety reasons. Unfortunately predators have access to public blogs too.)

By putting your thoughts, dreams, fears, opinions, and insights in a journal, you'll be able to record your senior year in black and white. While you assume you'll never forget what you're feeling and thinking today, you probably will. Years later, when you look back on this special time in your life, your journal will provide the details your mind has buried deep in storage somewhere.

Journaling is also quite therapeutic. It will help you sort through your thoughts, define how you really feel, and give you the words to articulate your ideas, fears, and conclusions. Sometimes your subconscious mind will even share secrets with you that you would never uncover in any other way.

Did you know that many professional writers got their start by writing in their journals? They thought they were just writing for their own benefit, but later they realized they had something to say to others as well. Not everything you write will be publishable, but some of it might be.

Journaling is a habit worth making and staying with. It can provide many hours of pleasant conversation with yourself and priceless memories told in your own words.

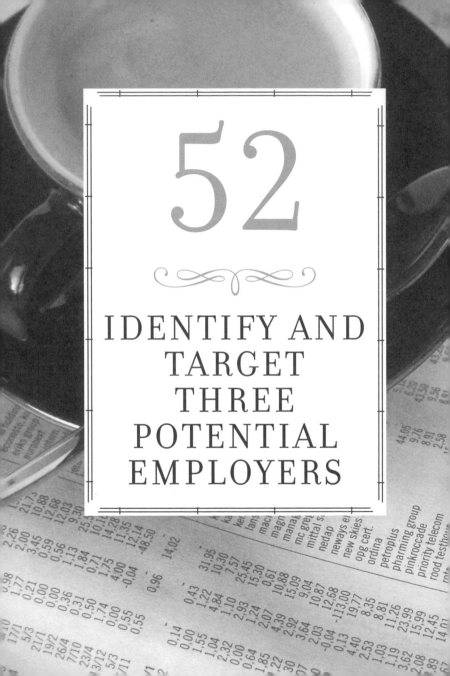

52

IDENTIFY AND
TARGET
THREE
POTENTIAL
EMPLOYERS

You may still be knee-deep in your education, but sooner or later you're going to be out there looking for a job. That's the tough part. Each employer is looking for the right person to fill his or her company's needs. Maybe he or she will choose you—maybe not. The fun part is that for now you get to do the choosing. Your options are fluid. You can target any company you find—and it's your needs, your interests, your dreams that are in the spotlight.

Even now, it's important to do your homework. Here are some helpful tips:

- Talk to your guidance counselor about desirable employers in your chosen field of study.
- Start reading the business section of the newspaper.
- Follow the stock market.
- Do drive-bys of local businesses you might be interested in working for one day.
- If you know people who already work for one of these companies, call and find out how satisfied they are, what kind of benefits they have, and their general likes and dislikes.

Target three companies or businesses of interest, and as you do your research, take notes. You may think your choices represent an impossible dream, but the truth is that all the people who work in those companies now were just like you once—students with ambitions and dreams. If they could get there, you can too. And preparing for it, knowing all you can, gives you a great advantage.

53

BEGIN TO THINK
OF TIME AS
INVESTMENT
CAPITAL

Oscar Wilde once said, "No man is rich enough to buy back his past." In other words, time is our most valuable asset. Once time is spent, you can never retrieve it, so use it wisely. You need to approach time in much the same way that you deal with money. Start thinking of it as an investment in your future. If you get a handle on the big T now, you'll become much more productive at whatever you do after graduation.

Of course, there are always going to be time stealers around to help you waste those precious minutes, so you have to be on guard. Television is one of the worst offenders. One sitcom leads to another and then another, and before you know it, the entire evening is gone and you have no idea where it went. While surfing the Web can be very beneficial and productive, it can also occupy a great deal of time. The telephone can rob you blind—especially if you have gabby friends. Even people themselves can suck up time like a sponge. Needy people can latch on for dear life, using up your time and energy, yet offering nothing in return. Yep, there are time stealers all around. So be wise and set boundaries.

To make the most of your time, it is a good idea to keep a daily "to do" list and a calendar planner to help organize the slices of time throughout your day. Don't become a prisoner to your list, but let it serve as a guide, helping you navigate your day. Prioritize your activities, remembering to schedule time for God, your family, your friends, and yourself.

Believe it or not, managing your time well gives you more of it— to do with as you please.

54

VERBALIZE

YOUR

DREAMS

Words have power. With them, God created the universe. It was with words that Jesus raised Lazarus from the dead. The Bible says this: "If you confess with your mouth, 'Jesus is Lord,' and believe in your heart that God raised him from the dead, you will be saved" (Romans 10:9). Words serve also as the currency for eternal life. In order to succeed, you must begin now to put into words your hopes and dreams for the future.

Begin by telling God about those things that are in your heart. Doesn't He already know? Of course He does. But He wants you to know. And He wants the opportunity to help you refine and prove them. Find a quiet, alone place where you can pray out loud. This is guaranteed to bring clarity and dimension to what before might have been only an impression.

You'll know when it's time to verbalize your dreams to others— your parents, friends, teachers, classmates. Wait until you feel comfortable that you've worked it out with God before you tell others. And be selective. Choose an appropriate time, make your presentation humbly but with passion, and then ask for input.

Once you've crossed that bridge, it's time to start verbally establishing your dreams. Repeat them to yourself out loud as often as you can each day. Listen to the words as you speak them. This will truly establish your determination to go the distance. Most of all, never forget that there is power in your words—power to make your dreams come true.

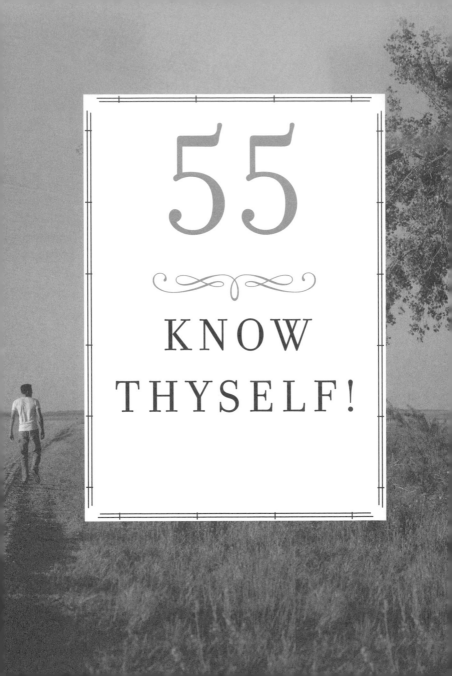

55

KNOW
THYSELF!

Did you know that the most difficult person to know is yourself? Does that surprise you? Most people see this truth only after it's pointed out. Then they begin to understand why they struggle with certain things more than others.

Unfortunately, it's very easy to lie to ourselves. We choose not to think that we're selfish when we push for our own way. We tell ourselves that we're doing the right thing, when we're really doing the thing we want to be right.

There is really just one way for us to know ourselves: by God's revelation. The Holy Spirit speaks directly to our hearts and shows us the error of our ways, the truth we can't bear to admit. Then He compassionately helps us to face ourselves and initiate reform.

This may sound like a painful process and often it is—but it's also a major advance on the road to success in every pursuit of life. If you know yourself—really know your weaknesses, such as your tendency to procrastinate or your misguided sense of entitlement—you can make informed choices, become more sensitive to others, and avoid walking blindly through life.

Now, not later, is the right time to begin this journey of personal enlightenment. Ask God to help you see yourself as you really are, and He'll do it—gently, one surprise at a time. He'll get you through it. And you'll move into the next phase of your life with an amazing advantage.

56

PUT IN YOUR FULL
EIGHT HOURS OF
SLEEP—AT LEAST
ONCE!

Are you getting enough sleep?

Probably not. Millions of people who live in this fast-paced world get six or fewer hours of sleep each night—and that is not enough, according to Dr. James B. Maas, author of *Power Sleep*. He says we've become a nation of walking zombies, with more than half of the U.S. adult population carrying a substantial sleep debt. And with late-night study sessions, too many assignments, and not enough hours to get everything done, students are also often way behind in their payments.

Consider these symptoms of sleep deprivation: daytime drowsiness, mood shifts, depression, irritability, loss of sense of humor, anxiety, poor coping skills, loss of interest in social interaction, weight gain, feeling chilled, reduced immunity to disease and viral infection, lethargy, reduced productivity, reduced ability to concentrate, impaired memory, reduced ability to handle complex tasks, reduced ability to think logically, and more.

Now here are nine strategies to help you drift off to dreamland:

* ❖ Exercise regularly—but not within three hours of going to bed.
* ❖ Eat a healthy diet.
* ❖ Keep mentally stimulated during the day.
* ❖ Clear your mind at bedtime.
* ❖ Try some bedtime relaxation techniques.
* ❖ Don't smoke.
* ❖ Reduce caffeine intake—especially close to bedtime.
* ❖ Take a warm bath before retiring for the night.
* ❖ Establish a bedtime ritual.

Things probably aren't going to slow down after you leave school, so getting in the habit of sleeping well and adequately is a wonderful investment for your happy and healthy future.

57

UPDATE
YOUR
ADDRESS
BOOK

I wish I knew how to get hold of Jenna. She was my best friend in economics and now I have no idea where she is. I think she might be in New York somewhere, but I didn't get her address or phone number there."

This will happen to you—it will—unless you take action now and get busy putting together your own little directory of friendly hearts. Set a goal to get the contact information of three friends each day until you have all of them recorded. Make sure you get their full names (it's a good idea to have these, even if they go by nicknames), current addresses, phone numbers for a land phone as well as a cell phone, e-mail addresses, and Web site addresses. It's also a good idea to get their parents' contact information since your friends will likely move several times over the next few years, while their parents probably won't. Also, if your friends already know where they'll be living after graduation, get that information, too, noting when they will begin living at that new address. Finally, you might also record your friends' birthdays, so you can keep in touch on those special days.

If you can pull it off, an information-sharing party is great fun. With everyone there, you can get it all done in one night and your friends can too. Have everyone bring a snack and make a night of it.

Too often we take the people in our lives for granted. We don't stop to think how we'll feel when they disappear from our lives. A friend is a terrible thing to waste.

58

READ FOR FUN!

I f you could compile every book, article, and handout you've been required to read so far, the stack would probably more than reach the ceiling. Even then, you might think it should be much higher. Learning is about reading really. But reading comes in many packages, and you'll find it helpful to mix some pleasure reading in with all the class materials.

Reading can be a release as well as an obligation. It can entertain you, relax you, cheer you up, make you laugh, spark an insight. It can take you away from your troubles, rest your mind, and help you see that the world is bigger than the information you've been eyeball to eyeball with for so long.

Of course, to read for fun, you can't be a book snob. You must be willing to pick up a paperback novel and float from one page to another without judgment, without analysis, without preconceived notions. Just read for the love of it. Lose yourself in the story. If you're not fond of fiction—though many would argue that their lives are not worth living without it—you can still find some pretty relaxing reads out there. Buy a bathroom reader, a joke book, or even the *Guinness Book of World Records*.

Reading, like breathing, should be a constant, daily element of your life. You won't be able to kiss it good-bye when you graduate—not if you hope to succeed, that is. Always make it a rule, though, to read for fun as well as duty. You'll be a brighter, more interesting, better-adjusted person for having done it.

59

~~~

TRY YOUR
HAND AT
SCHOOL
POLITICS

Maybe you've never aspired to be the next George W. Bush, but have you ever desired to see things improve on campus? Well, then school politics is the way to go. School government is a great way to learn about the political system as well as enhance your résumé a bit. Even if you don't win the title of class president or some other office, the fact that you had enough tenacity and spirit to run for such a noble position will earn you the admiration of many.

Call your school office and find out when the next elections will take place. Then fill out the appropriate paperwork so you can officially announce your candidacy. Enlist your best friends to help you organize your campaign, including a kickoff party to get things rolling. They could also help you come up with a catchy slogan that best describes you as a candidate and design a cool flier to hang up all over campus. For an added bit of advertising, have some "Vote for Pedro" type T-shirts made, and pass them out to your friends to wear.

When everything is in place, contact your campus newspaper and offer an interview with a sure winner. Invite your classmates to your kickoff bash. Last, but certainly not least, find out as much as you can about the current hot topics on campus and begin researching each one so that you can speak intelligently on any issue that might come up during the campaign.

Remember, running for office in not just about winning. Regardless of the outcome, it will be yet another experience to help you reach your full potential as you learn the ins and outs of politics. Win or lose, you'll be a winner for having had the guts to go for it!

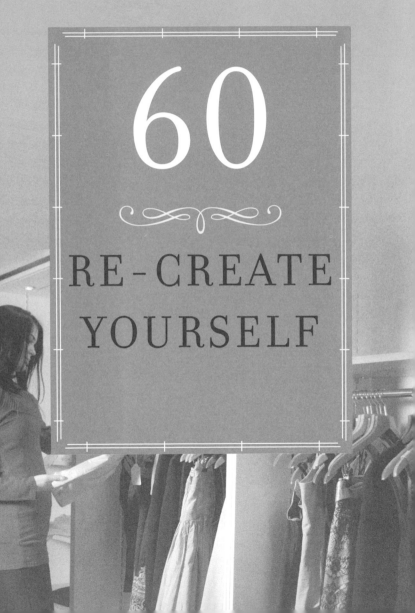

60

RE-CREATE YOURSELF

Soon you will be entering a new phase of your life. Whether that's heading off to college or jumping into the job market, it may be time to evaluate your current look and see if some changes need to be made.

This doesn't have to be expensive. Grab your best friend or someone who has his/her style together, and re-create yourself.

Start with basic things such as getting a manicure. Manicures are important for both women and men. Let's face it: dirty fingernails give the wrong message. And while you're in the spa, treat yourself to a pedicure too.

Next, hit the outlet mall or a department store and pick up some key accessories such as belts, shoes, handbags, briefcases, scarves, and jewelry. New accessories can totally update your wardrobe. They can also stretch it, giving a black suit several different looks with the simple change of a scarf or tie.

Of course, you'll also want to take an honest look at your current hairstyle. Is it outdated? If so, opt for a classic style—one that works on weekends as well as more formal occasions. Guys? You might explore some hair gel and spike your hair a bit for a different look.

Let's not forget good breath and nice teeth. Make an appointment with your dentist to get your teeth cleaned and ask about a whitening treatment. If you can't afford a whitening treatment in the dental office, opt for an over-the-counter one, available at most discount stores. A bright, white smile is the best accessory you can have.

Last, practice making a good impression with a firm handshake. This is an important step on your road to success.

61

VOLUNTEER
TO BABYSIT

A s if you needed something else on your already-full plate, right? But babysitting is too good to pass up. You can have fun, have a quiet place to study (after your young charges are off to bed), and you can make money while you're doing it.

If you're not sure of your babysitting skills, you can take a course through your local chapter of the American Red Cross. It's always a good idea to know child and infant CPR before agreeing to babysit—just in case you ever need it. This will also go a long way toward reassuring parents that they can safely leave their precious little ones in your care.

Babysitting can also be a lovely gift for someone—a teacher you'd like to thank or a single parent who needs a break. Many of the best gifts cost only your time and effort and babysitting is truly a gift from the heart.

But if you think those are all the benefits, you're wrong. This job is like real-time practice for the adult world. It requires caring, sensitivity, alertness, insight, problem-solving skills, creativity, stamina, crowd management, good judgment, courage, determination, the ability to multitask, people skills—and that's a very incomplete list. Babysitting is just an accelerated course in life skills—including the ones you'll need when you have children of your own one day.

62

ATTEND A
RÉSUMÉ-
WRITING
SEMINAR

Your résumé is a primary tool for presenting yourself to the world at large. It's your calling card, your first impression. You can see how important it is to get it right. Long before you put in a bid for that first big professional job, you'll need it in some form to apply for specialized part-time employment, high school and college internships and scholarships, college applications and certain courses of study, high school and college foreign study, and contests, to name only a few. Start working on yours long before graduation.

A seminar is often a good idea for learning how to prepare a dynamic résumé. You can find one online or through your guidance counselor. Many of them are free.

The following tips can help you craft the best possible résumé:

1. Keep it short. Try to keep the description of your education, skills, experience, and awards to one page.

2. Be direct. Be specific about the duties you have performed. Don't just state what your job description was.

3. Be relevant! Adapt your résumé to fit the application you're responding to.

4. Be truthful! Many people can't resist the temptation to embellish their credentials. This is a bad idea. If found out, you could lose an important scholarship or internship, even get fired.

5. Finally, make it attractive. Use high-quality paper and a good printer. Your commitment to excellence will be reflected in the details.

Time spent creating a great résumé will definitely pay off—and sooner than you think.

63

OPEN A
SAVINGS
ACCOUNT

S ave what?

That's a fairly reasonable response for a person in school to the idea of a savings account. You don't have a lot of money as it is, and putting it in an account where it will earn the whopping windfall of two to three dollars a year just seems crazy. If it was all about the interest, you'd be right—but is it?

Actually, opening an account for saving is about much more than the measly interest you would earn. It's about setting a precedent in your life. It's about developing a lifelong policy of living on less than what you have—rather than more. It's an exercise in thrift and good stewardship. It demonstrates a proactive approach to your future.

All that?

Oh yes, and more.

Many people go through life living from paycheck to paycheck. They never seem to get ahead and have little or nothing to show for their hard work. They often don't even know what becomes of their hard-earned dollars. But the person who nurtures a "savings mentality" learns how to plug the hole at the bottom of the bucket, simply by paying attention and setting priorities.

If you're just sure you have no money for savings, buy yourself a change bank—one that will sort and package your change. Get in the habit of dropping all your loose change in the bank each night. Keep the rolled change in a shoe box in the closet and don't touch it until you have about fifty dollars. (This will happen sooner than you think.) Then use it to open your account and watch it grow.

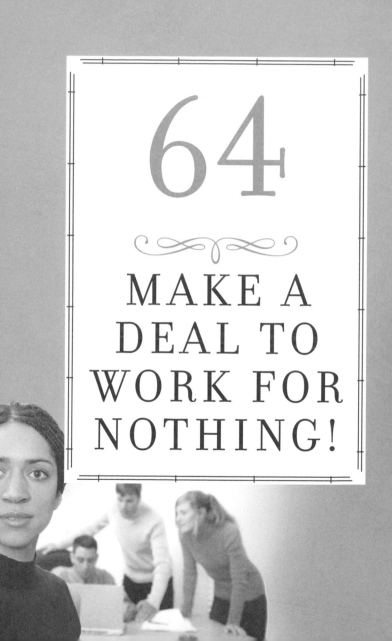

64

MAKE A DEAL TO WORK FOR NOTHING!

W ork for nothing? That doesn't sound too wise, does it? Actually, it is one of the smartest things you can do! Internships provide on-the-job training while helping you get your foot in the door of a company that might not otherwise look at you because of your lack of experience. In addition, some internships earn valuable credits toward graduation, so make sure you look into that aspect as well.

Another big advantage is that you will be able to "try out" your career without having to make a long-term commitment. If you find you love it, you'll be that much closer to making it a paying reality.

You will also find that internships provide important contacts within the company and sometimes in the industry as a whole. These valuable relationships can often get you a letter of recommendation or insider information about job openings.

The best way to get yourself noticed once you get in the door is to be willing to do anything asked of you. If you're asked to make coffee, do it. If someone needs copies made or materials collated, handle it. You'll soon be noticed and that will lead to opportunities to help with more interesting projects.

Over all, internships are a win/win situation for both students and employers. Employers benefit by having low-cost labor from enthusiastic, knowledgeable students, as well as the opportunity to connect with potentially future paid employees. It's no wonder that so many companies participate in such programs.

Both high school and college guidance counselors keep lists of available internships. Drop by and check them out.

65

STAY UP ALL NIGHT—TO TALK

You want a real memory, something you can tuck away in your heart forever? Try staying up all night and welcoming in the morning with a good friend.

Pick a perfect night, spread out a blanket, and relax under the stars. Be sure to talk and laugh and reminisce about good times you've had together. Share the dreams you have for the future. It will be a special time for both of you—guaranteed.

Identify the various star constellations, and share something with your friend that you've never told anyone else. Talk about first dates, first kisses, and first loves. Talk about nothing. If you're there with a truly great friend, the conversation will never feel forced. It will just flow—all night long.

Welcome the morning sunrise with a very special conversation—a prayer. In the beauty of the moment, thank God together for His goodness. Thank Him for the sunrise, your friendship, the journey that lies ahead. You'll be tired but it will be worth it, and much more memorable than staying up all night writing a paper or cramming for a test.

In the years to come, you'll always cherish those moments. And who knows, you may have an opportunity to repeat your all-nighter much farther down the road.

In a world of e-mails and fax machines, we often underestimate the intimacy that comes from simple, unrushed conversation. It's in those encounters that we show our hearts and establish bonds. Tell someone you care about that you want to keep him or her close forever. Then set the stage to do just that.

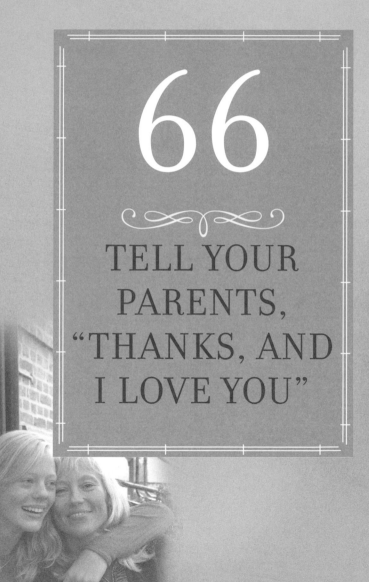

66

TELL YOUR PARENTS, "THANKS, AND I LOVE YOU"

There's an excellent chance that one day you'll have children, and when you do, you'll understand why it seems so natural to always put your children ahead of yourself, make sacrifices for them, love and care for them without any thought of being compensated for your efforts. Parents possess a God-given instinct to cherish their offspring. In a very real sense they can't help themselves. They probably aren't expecting you to say "Thank you," but they will very much appreciate it when you do.

It doesn't have to be a fancy, formal form of thanks. The words are the important part, much more important than how they're delivered. Just tell them—together or separately—how much their love and support have meant to you. When they shrug it off as nothing (most parents will), press in and mention some specifics. "Thanks, Mom, for encouraging me to stick with piano. I almost quit so many times, but you were always there to give me a push back in the right direction. My music means so much to me now, and somehow you knew it would be. I appreciate it." Or you might say, "Thanks, Dad, for shelling out all that cash so I could play football. I realize now just how hard it must have been to come up with the money. I appreciate it."

Let words of appreciation become a way of life for you—now and after graduation. Set a pattern of thankfulness. Don't just wait for a special occasion to say what's on your heart. Seize the day, and surprise your parents with genuine words of gratitude. You'll definitely make their day.

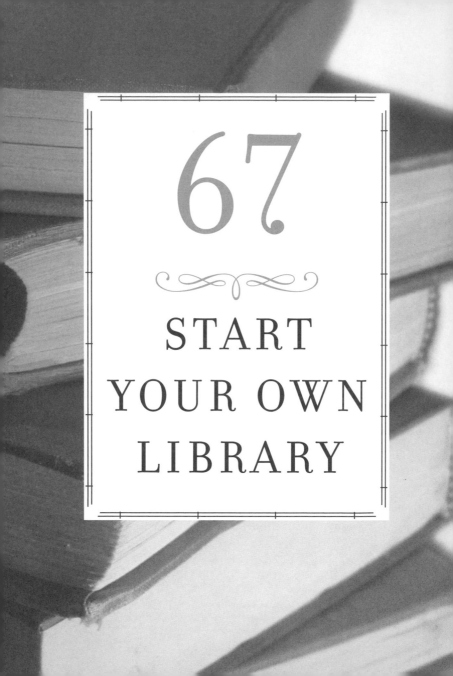

67

START YOUR OWN LIBRARY

As a student, you may have collected a ton of books over the years. Now is the time to go through them, discard the ones you won't need, and pack up the ones you'll want to keep—the makings of your very first personal library.

There are several ways to get rid of the books you don't need and even make a little money. You can sell them to used-book stores or have a yard sale and mark your unwanted literature one and two dollars per item. College textbooks can be sold back to the bookstore. Now you have room for some appropriate additions.

Start by adding the classics—Dickens, Tolstoy, Joyce, Austen, Twain, Faulkner, Lawrence, Hardy, Hemingway, Brontë, Morrison, and others. Also be on the lookout for books in a variety of genres— children's books, biographies, historical fiction, novels, nonfiction, etc. Let the *New York Times* Best Sellers list and Publishers Weekly guide your choices. And be sure to keep the books, even by no-name authors, that you particularly enjoy.

No need to be in a hurry. Just have fun looking for them at thrift stores, garage sales, and half-price bookstores.

You'll also want to add books pertinent to your future profession. Many professional books cost big bucks, so check out *overstock.com*, *eBay*, and *amazon.com* before you pay full price at your local bookstore. And for the really pricey titles? Put them on your gift wish list and let your family and friends bless you with them for Christmas, your birthday, and graduation. As you hone your reading collection and build your library, you'll be investing in a lifetime of reading pleasure.

68

SET A DATE FOR A RENDEZVOUS

L ong before graduation, you and your friends will begin to make plans for what comes after—more schooling, jobs, marriage. Most will move away. Don't wait until you're all crying and hugging and making empty promises to each other. Start now to plant the idea of a reunion rendezvous at some point in the future.

You're more apt to get everyone on board if you include everyone in the planning. Host a cozy little party to preplan an event everyone will enjoy. Set a date, even if it's a couple of years down the road, and decide what you want to do together and where. Dream your little hearts out. This might be as simple as coming home for a football game at your alma mater next year or as fancy as meeting on the beach in Maui five years after graduation.

You make it real by reinforcing it with your friends every chance you get. Talk about it; try to imagine how much fun it will be. Keep up the pep talk before, during, and after you graduate. When the big date finally arrives, everyone won't be there, but even if just a few of you make it, you'll have a wonderful, nostalgic time—one that will remind you of younger years and reestablish cherished relationships.

Make it a priority to keep your friendships going—no matter the time or distance. One day you will be so glad you did. And just think—you'll have something special to look forward to together.

69

GO OUT
ON A LIMB

Do you dream of doing something daring, something far-out? Maybe that's skydiving or bungee jumping. You might want to take a trip alone. Whatever it is, quit dreaming and start planning. Before you graduate, go out on a limb and do something you've never done before.

It might mean working ahead in a few of your classes, but the effort will have a big payoff. It will give you renewed confidence and a sense of personal accomplishment. It could be just the impetus you need to get you through that last difficult year. Most of all, it will teach you that taking an occasional calculated risk is essential to success.

Take time to plan your daring activity well. Go online and find out where, when, and what it will cost. You may even want to pay a visit to a travel agent or the skydiving school—whatever the site of your adventure might be. Doing your homework will help your excitement grow—and you will probably need that to keep yourself on track.

If your daring dream requires travel, you may have to wait until summer, but don't wait until the summer after you graduate—it's already too crowded with changes. Get it done before you throw your mortarboard in the air. You'll need to save your money too. Daring deeds are rarely free.

Whatever limb you decide to climb out on—do it with gusto, knowing that it will help you become a calculated risk taker in the future.

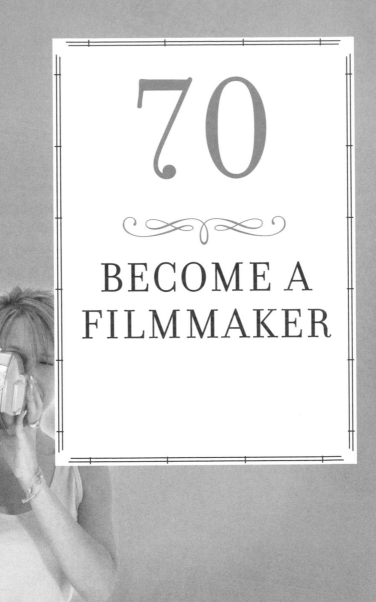

70

BECOME A
FILMMAKER

I f a picture is worth a thousand words, a video must be worth ten thousand! If you don't own a video camera, borrow or rent one. It's time to get campus life down on film.

It's best to capture your friends in their natural habitat. If your buddy Joel is a great Frisbee football player, interview him after a big game. If your friend Suzanne is working around the clock on the yearbook, catch her behind her desk with a red pen in her hand.

To make your movie even better, use humor. For instance, if your friend Nancy is known for her messy room, get it all on film and create some funny dialogue to go along with the footage. Add whimsical aspects to the film, such as "interviewing" your friends' pets about their owners. Comments from teachers and other faculty members are always entertaining! Interview your friends about your friends. And don't forget to capture group interaction. That's the best part—how you all are when you're together. If you make it a casual kind of thing, they won't even notice after a while.

If you want to get really creative, you might need some additional equipment to accomplish the moviemaking task at hand. Let's say you want to include a lot of action and your handheld shots look pretty amateurish upon review. Then you probably need a cam stabilizer to get that silky smooth footage.

Most importantly, just have fun. Capture meaningful footage of your friends and then make copies for everyone in your gang (an excellent idea for a graduation gift). You'll be happy you took the time to preserve memories, and so will they!

71

MANAGE
CREDIT
CARDS
WISELY

S tudents have become a primary target for credit card companies. But without the proper skills to use their cards judiciously, students often find themselves drowning in debt. It's never too early to learn to manage a credit card before it begins to manage you.

If you must have a card, be selective. Choose only one—the one with the lowest interest rate and credit limit. Then observe these guidelines:

❖ The word *emergency* is relative. Decide in advance what constitutes an actual emergency. Do not use it for anything else, no matter how tempting.

❖ Don't keep the card in your wallet. Put it in a safe place where you can get it if you need it but won't be tempted to use it on the spur of the moment.

❖ Pay off any balance every month. If you can't do that because of an especially large charge for a real emergency, don't charge anything additional until the balance is cleared.

A credit card can be useful as long as it's managed properly. It can help you secure a rental car, travel with a greater degree of peace of mind, and cover some of the unexpected eventualities of life. It can even help you build a sound credit rating before you launch out on your own.

Take the good a credit card can offer and refuse to get trapped by the bad. Your future is in your hands.

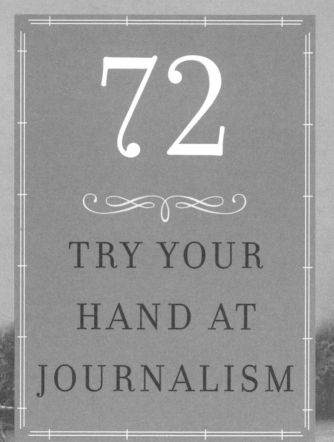

72

TRY YOUR
HAND AT
JOURNALISM

B efore you graduate, try your hand at some journalistic endeavor. That will probably be offered in the form of the school newspaper or yearbook. But it can also include campus radio and television stations. No matter what shape your life takes after graduation, you will be better off for having participated.

In most cases, getting started is as easy as deciding where you would like to get involved and then applying. Opportunities are available in photography, writing, design, marketing, and public relations. You can learn to conduct an interview, write an article, review a book, movie, or play, or report on a meeting or event.

These pursuits can lead to part-time employment, scholarships, and internships for both high-school and college students. They can also lead to stellar career opportunities. And they can be a lot of fun—like the time spent gathering material for the yearbook or covering the big game on the radio.

Avoid the mistake of thinking journalism is just for the editorially elite. Step up and see how it can work for you.

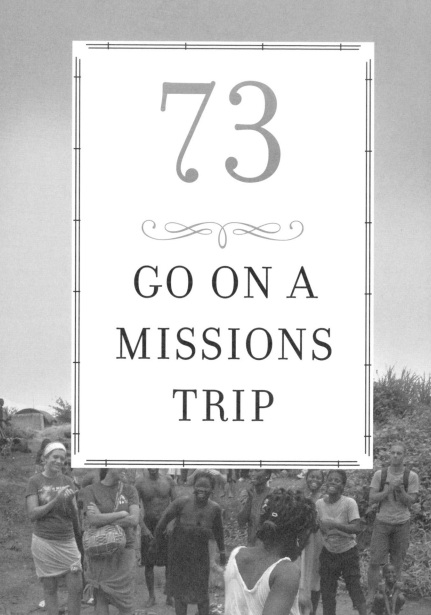

73

GO ON A MISSIONS TRIP

Every summer, groups across America head for unfamiliar soil to serve their fellow men and women. Some dig wells and plant crops; others build churches and feed the hungry. It's an experience that will change your worldview and make you more sensitive to the needs of others. And learning to serve others will open doors of compassion and empathy that you will find deeply satisfying—and possibly addictive.

These trips will take planning, and you will be responsible for your expenses. Some groups hold fund-raisers, but saving up your money and paying your own way is much more gratifying.

You should be careful not to jump at the first trip you hear about. Do some research and decide what kind of trip best fits your gifts and talents. Look for a country that truly interests you. An interest in the people and culture will cause you to be more effective and enjoy the trip more.

If you aren't able or willing to leave the U.S., all is not lost. There are countless opportunities to serve right here in America. Choose a relief organization and volunteer to help out right here in the States.

Life is too short to be lived solely for ourselves. We live best when we serve best. Given the amount of suffering and lack in the world at large, you will find many ways to help others while you're becoming a broader and more mature person.

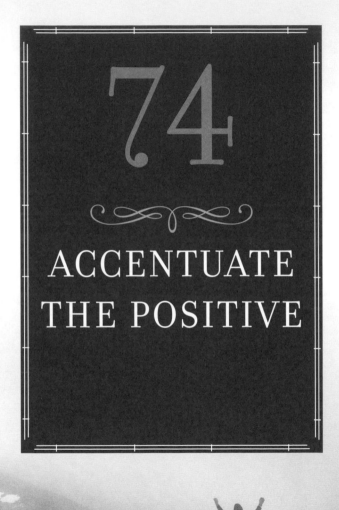

74

ACCENTUATE
THE POSITIVE

S o, are you a "glass half empty" or "glass half full" kind of person? If you have a hard time looking on the bright side, it's time to practice living in the positive before you become a Danny Downcast or Nellie Negative.

Positive thinking can have quite an effect on your overall performance and personality. Athletes have known this for a long time, which is why they spend hours visualizing themselves winning. Although many people leave athletics behind when they graduate, most often they carry the positive attitudes with them, clearly giving them an advantage in whatever they pursue. Whether or not we're into sports, it's a lesson we can all learn.

For some people, this will be a great challenge. Even for the person "born negative," however, improvement can be made over time. When a negative thought hits you, consciously begin to consider its positive counterpart. Counter "I'm so stupid. I'm sure I'm going to fail that exam" with the opposite thought: "I'm well prepared and God is helping me. There is no way I can fail."

This isn't just a good idea; it's a God idea. The Bible instructs us to think on good things. Think about all the wonderful, uplifting, encouraging things in your life. Meditate on God's promises to you—there are lots of them in the Bible. Stay focused on the bright side and ditch Danny Downcast and Nellie Negative for good! They aren't any fun anyway. Besides, there's a great big glorious world out there to enjoy!

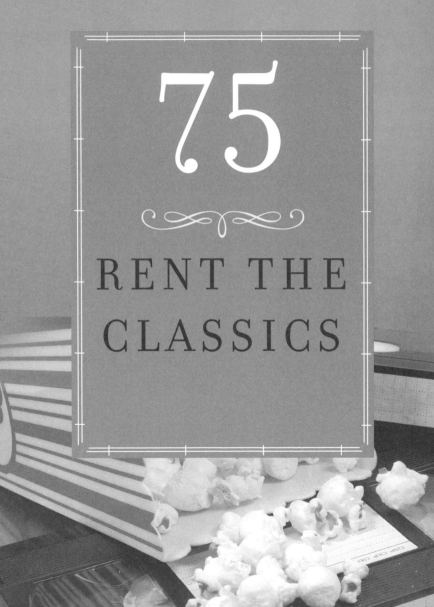

75

RENT THE
CLASSICS

There are movies and then there are *movies!*

Of course there are some wonderful newer films, but most depend more heavily on action and special effects than they do on intriguing plots and exceptional acting. Many older films, though often less technically sophisticated, are rich in character and context. The next time you chill out with a rental, make it a golden oldie and lose yourself in cinematic magic.

These suggested films are enthralling—even on a regular-sized television:

- *Arsenic and Old Lace*
- *Adam's Rib*
- *Gone with the Wind*
- *Casablanca*
- *The African Queen*
- *Now, Voyager*
- *The Grapes of Wrath*
- *Little Women*
- *Citizen Kane*
- *Ben Hur*
- *The Four Feathers*

This is a most inadequate list, of course, intended only to give you some good choices to begin with. Most video stores have a classics section with very reasonable fees. Once you've discovered this treasure, watch the classics again and again and revel in their soulful stories.

76

HAVE
AN ALL-
CHOCOLATE
DAY!

I magine this: an entire day filled with chocolate. How amazing would that be? You start the day with a steaming cup of decadent hot chocolate with frothy marshmallows on top, accompanied by a chocolate-covered doughnut. Then for lunch, a thick chocolate milkshake (topped with whipped cream and a cherry) with a cheeseburger (because you might need some protein). For a midday snack, pour yourself a tall glass of chocolate milk and open a pack of Oreos! For dinner . . . let's see . . . how about a big bowl of chocolate-covered strawberries—and a side salad? (Just make sure you throw on some chocolate-covered raisins for good measure.) Finish the evening with chocolate-covered peanuts and a large diet soda (you know, to balance it all out).

While you're enjoying your day of chocolate, don't feel the least bit guilty about it. Why? Because in limited amounts, chocolate is actually good for you. According to recent scientific studies, chocolate has many benefits.

- ❖ It causes a feeling of happiness: scientists have proven that it releases endorphins (naturally occurring feel-good chemicals) that enhance your mood.
- ❖ It is good for your heart. A study by the American Dietetic Association shows that chocolate (especially dark chocolate) can reduce the risk of heart disease. It seems the antioxidants in cocoa help prevent the buildup of fatty deposits in coronary arteries.
- ❖ The antioxidants in cocoa appear to reduce the risk of blood clots.

Don't hold back! Enjoy an all-chocolate day! Make it a solitary activity or invite the gang to join you—unless you're one of those people who simply can't share their chocolate.

77

PRACTICE
PEOPLE
WATCHING

I f you can get past your mother's childhood admonition not to stare, you will find that people watching is a fascinating pastime with some surprising benefits. Try it when you find yourself waiting for the doctor, the dentist, the bus, your flight, or your order. You might be surprised to find that what you'll see is funnier than any sitcom on television.

People are incredibly funny even when they don't intend to be—and completely unique. No two people walk alike, talk alike, or express themselves in just the same way. Watching them simply going about their business can turn a routine day into a day of high humor.

It can be totally hilarious to keep a small notebook in your purse for sketching unusual (bizarre) hairstyles, describing odd behavior, and noting heart-stopping color combinations.

Watching people walk their dogs can be the funniest of all, especially when dog and owner bear a striking resemblance.

People watching can certainly provide some much needed laughs. Of course, you could always use those waiting minutes to nap, but then you'd miss all the fun!

78

"HEY, EVERYBODY! LET'S HAVE A PICNIC!"

What could be better than a sunny afternoon, fresh air, good food, and a break from dark halls and class-rooms?

You could go to the trouble to plan your picnic outing, but why would you want to? Keep an old blanket in your car or locker, and when the sun opens its arms and bids you come, grab your friends, tell them to bring their bologna and tuna-salad sandwiches, fast-food hamburgers and tacos, and meet at the park. Spread out your blankets, and you've got everything you need for a sun-drenched minibreak from the everyday stress of school.

Once you're settled, eat slowly, enjoying each bite, and relish the comfort of being with people who like you just the way you are. Feel the sun on your skin, the breeze in your hair, and then lie back, close your eyes, and take a short nap—or throw around a Frisbee or a football.

The truth is that these spontaneous get-togethers are often as memorable, if not more, than the high-maintenance, heavy-cleanup kind. Just make sure you have a camera to chronicle the event.

School can be especially stressful as you approach those last months before graduation: so many things must be decided, missed courses made up, finals studied for, end-of-term papers completed, transcripts finalized. Those lunches in the park will help you bond with your best friends and serve as sunny stress-busters as the semester winds down.

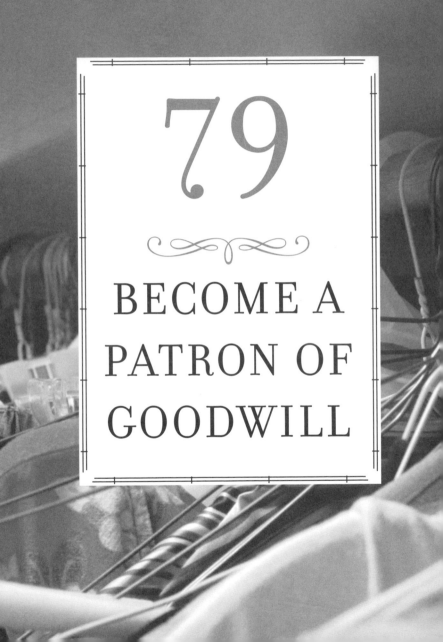

79

BECOME A
PATRON OF
GOODWILL

Whether you're furnishing your bedroom at home, a college dorm room, or your apartment, you can find some really cool stuff at your area Goodwill store. Here's a tip: flip through some home decorating magazines and find a look you like. Then, tear out that page and carry it with you on your shopping excursion. Look for pieces similar to the ones featured in the picture you have. Rather than pay twenty-five dollars for a laundry basket, get the same look and quality for two or three dollars. The picture will give you a guide so you won't feel overwhelmed while shopping for good buys and good looks. From eclectic furniture pieces to brand-new lamps and bedding—thrift stores truly have something for every taste.

Along with furniture, thrift stores like Goodwill also carry brand-name clothing at bargain prices. You can dress like a million bucks and spend only a few. The savvy shopper also knows that these are the best places of all to put together a unique look and find retro fashions.

In fact, you can find almost anything at these stores: books, bedding, dishes, rugs, party supplies, shoes, jackets, toys, and much more.

Bargain shopping is a skill that everyone needs. But many people choose thrift stores not because they have to but because they want to. They like the idea of shrinking their necessary spending and expanding their discretionary cash. Once you treat yourself to the thrill of a thrifty purchase, it's tough to go back to department store prices.

80

PAMPER
YOURSELF

Sure, it would be nice if you could book a package at a nearby spa and be pampered all day long. But that can be quite expensive. So why not pamper yourself in the luxury of your own place?

After you've finished an important exam with hours of studying, depriving yourself of sleep, and eating cold pizza, you deserve some "me time." So just do it! Go to your local dollar store and purchase a few key items: an aromatherapy candle (lavender is a calming scent), some bath beads or crystals, some body lotion (make sure it matches the scent of your candle and bath beads), a CD of relaxing music or sounds of nature, and a bath pillow (a rolled-up fluffy towel will serve the same purpose).

Start by treating yourself to a meal of your favorite carryout. Follow it up with a cup of hot tea or cocoa and spend some time leisurely reading your Bible to feed your spirit. Your CD playing in the background will create an atmosphere conducive to relaxation. Next, treat yourself to that luxurious bath and follow it up with a facial.

This probably won't do it for you guys, but there is no shortage of ways you can pamper yourself as well. Spend a whole Saturday playing golf or video games. Put on your favorite music while you take a five-hour nap. Throw a football around outside.

The objective is to be kind to yourself. Do all of the things you've wanted to do on those days when you were too busy to turn around. God wants us to take care of our bodies, our spirits, and our souls. After all, they are the temple of the Holy Spirit. So do some temple maintenance and enjoy some pampering. You're worth it!

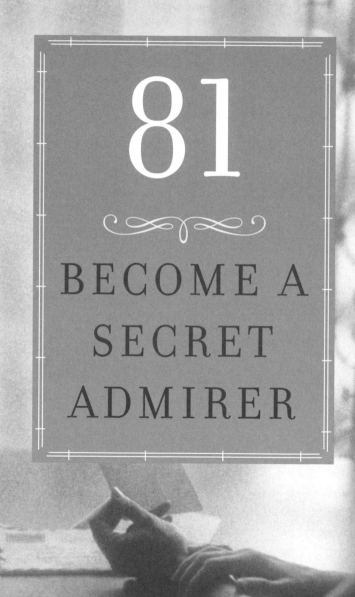

81

BECOME A SECRET ADMIRER

There's nothing like a compliment to brighten your day. When someone says, "You have a gorgeous smile," or "That's a great haircut," or "You are such a good friend"—you can't help but feel wonderful. But guess what? You'll feel just as wonderful if you're the one giving the compliments—maybe even better!

Choose someone in your life whom you want to flood with compliments, and become that person's secret admirer for a week. Get creative! Here are some ideas to get you started.

- ❖ Bake a batch of cookies and leave them somewhere your "admired person" will find them. Leave a note that says, "Just because you're special."
- ❖ Send an anonymous letter saying something like, "Just wanted you to know that you inspire me to be a better person. You truly are a gift from God."
- ❖ Write compliments on sticky notes and put them on the door to the person's room.
- ❖ Have a song on the radio dedicated to him or her, when you know he or she will be listening.
- ❖ Leave a chocolate bar in an appropriate place with a note that says, "Your smile is sweeter than candy."
- ❖ Ask God to bless that person with hope, joy, and peace each day.

The Bible urges us to encourage one another. It also tells us to do unto others as we would like others to do unto us. In essence, becoming someone's secret admirer isn't just a good idea, it's also a biblical principle. Go ahead and compliment away! The gift will bless the giver most.

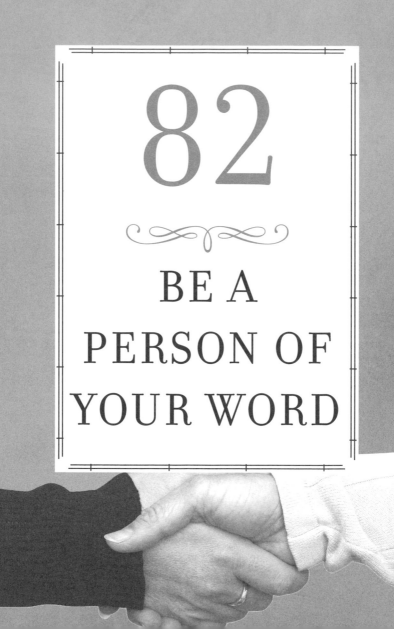

82

BE A PERSON OF YOUR WORD

I t's been a long time since a person's handshake was all it took to secure a deal. Today, forms must be signed in triplicate. It seems that people just don't trust each other anymore, and for good reason. Contracts are broken on a regular basis. People default on loans and don't think a thing about it. Many break their vows.

Even though times have changed, one thing remains the same: integrity is a person's best calling card. Are you a person of integrity? When you give your word, do people believe you? If not, now is the time to start rewriting your script and making good on your words.

To excel in an area takes practice. Becoming a person of integrity is a lifelong endeavor. So if you're ready for the challenge, here are some tips for becoming that person you desire.

- ❖ Always go the extra mile in the name of integrity. Exceed the expectations of others.
- ❖ Respect others by being on time.
- ❖ If you say you're going to do something, do it—when you say you will.
- ❖ Think carefully before giving your word. Then keep it at all costs.
- ❖ Never pass the buck. Accept responsibility.

The seed of integrity is on the inside of you. Maybe you've neglected it for a while, but it's there. Just give it some attention and watch it blossom. It will take you far in life—both personally and professionally.

83

~~~~~~~~~~

TAKE A PASS
ON ALCOHOL,
DRUGS, AND
SEX

They start preaching the "Just Say No" message when you're in elementary school, yet many choose not to heed the warning. If you've made it this far without venturing into the world of alcohol, drugs, and premarital sex, you are already on the road to success—and sadly, in the minority.

If you've wavered here and there over the years, don't beat yourself up. Just start over again. That's the great thing about God. When you tell Him you're sorry for your mistakes, He wipes the slate clean and even forgets what you did! It's like hitting the restart button on your video game. It's a whole new beginning! Today is your new day.

Be sure to steer clear of temptation—and there is plenty of it! Choose friends who are also determined to say no. That may mean that you have to keep your distance from someone you really like. It's unfortunate, but wisdom demands it. Be careful about where you go. For the most part, you're aware of where the danger spots are, which parties are likely to include drinking, what groups encourage drug use. If you find yourself in an awkward position you didn't expect—leave! It's that simple.

Being young and fun-loving is good—derailing your future is not. Be strong and steadfast in your stance against drugs, alcohol, and premarital sex. The choices, good and bad, that you make today will be felt for the rest of your life.

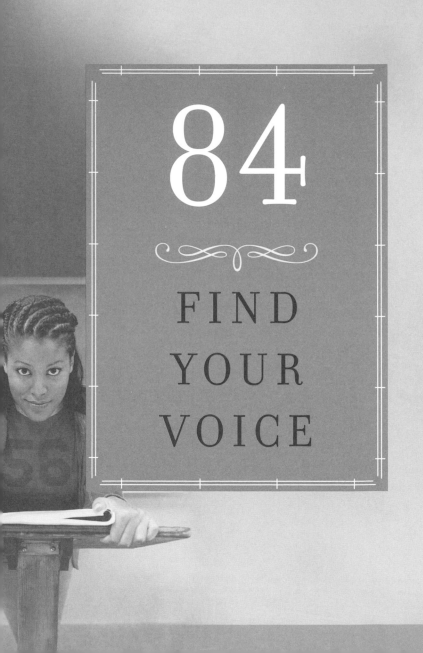

84

FIND
YOUR
VOICE

Assertiveness isn't the same thing as being pushy. Assertiveness means standing up for your rights and not being taken advantage of, while being pushy means standing up for your rights but violating the rights of others in the process. There's a big difference.

Being assertive also means being able to communicate articulately, to say what you want to say without fear, to verbalize a raw, honest expression of your heart. It takes practice, but you can learn how to do it. Sure, you may have sweaty palms at first, but you can be assertive. Here are some tips:

- ❖ Use a calm, level tone of voice. When you begin to shout, people begin to close their ears.
- ❖ Be honest but respectful. Rude, disrespectful behavior will cause you to lose credibility. Even if what you have to say is brilliant, people will not take you seriously. They may even discredit your remarks simply because they feel threatened by your demeanor.
- ❖ Don't equivocate. Say what you mean and mean what you say.
- ❖ Maintain direct eye contact. Your body language often speaks louder than your words.
- ❖ Make a point of remaining relaxed and open, no matter how the other person responds. If you lose your head, you lose.
- ❖ Make sure your facial expression agrees with what you are saying. Mixed signals will always weaken your position.
- ❖ Be bold, even if your knees are knocking. Never allow fear to steal your voice.

Your opinions and beliefs count. Ask God to help you gain the confidence to stand up for yourself and your beliefs.

85

FEED THE
HUNGRY

Have you ever been hungry? Sure. Everyone has. You might miss a meal or two if you're really busy or focused on something else. But as soon as you break free from what you're doing, your stomach tells you it's tired of waiting. That growling, churning sensation says, "Feed me!" And you do!

But what if simply walking to the refrigerator or going through a takeout line isn't an option? What if there is no way to feed your hunger? That's what millions of people around the world face each day. War, famine, disaster, disease, poverty—any one of these can leave millions thinking of nothing other than how they can quiet their screaming bodies.

You might be thinking that these people live far beyond your reach in some foreign land—and many do. But others live nearby. You can see them most every day if you're looking. Ask God to open your eyes to the hungry around you. He will!

Charities feed hundreds of thousands of people both at home and abroad through donations. Many organizations allow you to sponsor a child or family financially. Your church could support and staff a soup kitchen or local food bank for the needy. There is a constant need for volunteers at such places to stock shelves, prepare food, or deliver groceries and meals.

On several occasions Jesus stopped preaching long enough to feed the multitudes who were following Him through the countryside. The Bible says He had compassion on them because they were hungry. Will you reach out with compassion to the hungry around you?

86

❧

WHEREVER
YOU ARE—BE
ALL THERE

Have you ever gotten so focused on a goal that you forgot to enjoy the journey? It's easy to do, but think how much of life we miss out on if we live only for the end result. If you're always looking ahead to the next goal, you're bound to miss some beautiful scenery along the way. It's okay to be goal-oriented as long as you don't let your future consume your today. Live in the moment!

Share a pizza with your best friend. Take time to hug your mom and dad or call just to talk. Read the book you've been wanting to read, stop to smell a flower or admire a tree, go for a swim, bake cookies, hang out with your buddies, live your life—not just later, but now. Squeeze every drop of goodness out of each moment and thank God for the privilege of greeting each new day with a smile.

As you prepare for graduation and ultimately the next phase of your life, don't let the necessary planning stop you from being *all* there. You get today only once. Don't waste it. Jesus gave some good advice. He said, "Don't be anxious about tomorrow. God will take care of your tomorrow too. Live one day at a time" (Matt. 6:34 TLB).

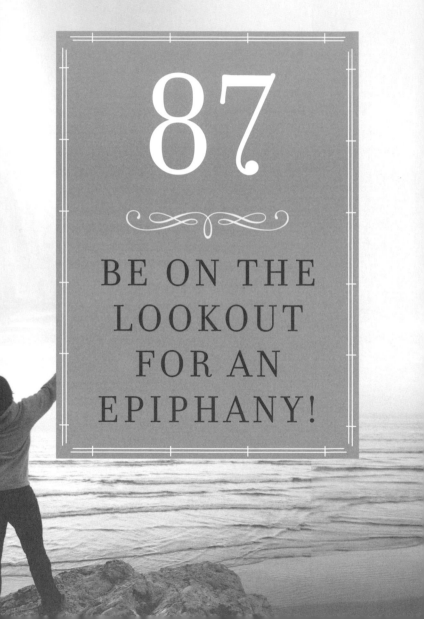

87

BE ON THE LOOKOUT FOR AN EPIPHANY!

There are moments in life that make us say, "Aha!" Those Eureka-type experiences define who we are. They change us. They inspire us to do other things. They make us evaluate our lives. The key is to recognize those moments in life, appreciate them, and remember them.

Laurie Henry, author of *The Fiction Dictionary*, defines *epiphanies* like this: "A sudden moment of insight when a character discovers some truth important to the story." It's the same way in real life—the telling of your story. There are moments of awakening so monumental that they make you stop and think, "Wow. That's awesome. I never thought of it that way." You discover a truth that changes you—forever.

Think back on your life. Can you identify some of those epiphanies? Maybe you've been so busy with exams and planning for the next phase of your life that you haven't been struck by any lately. Well, it's not too late. Make a conscious effort to open your mind to those "aha!" moments, and pretty soon they'll be flowing again.

Be sure, when they do come, that you write them down. It would be a good idea to keep a notebook designated just for that purpose. That way you can read them and cogitate on them until they become part of who you are.

Graduation will come and go, but learning will be a constant throughout your life, whatever you do. Don't miss any of those delightful awakenings of understanding.

88

INVITE YOUR FRIENDS TO A LATE-NIGHT SNACK BUFFET

Have you ever raided the refrigerator at midnight? A hoagie sandwich with lots of mustard. A big tub of popcorn with lots of butter. A dozen or so Hershey Kisses. Some pepperoni pizza. Ice cream out of the carton. Mmmm! The only thing that tastes better than a late-night snack is a late-night snack with friends. While you're all still together, schedule a Grab a Bite at Night party with your best buds!

You could purchase one of those extra-long submarine sandwiches—an especially good choice if your pals are health conscious. But if your buddies are sweet-tooth types, pull out all the stops and host a decadent dessert buffet. From chocolate-chip cookies to double-chocolate cheesecake to strawberry shortcake—greet sunrise on a sugar high. Is your mouth watering yet?

Maybe your friends just love to pig out. If so, try a finger-food buffet featuring teeny weenies, sweet and sour meatballs, chicken tenders, buffalo wings, veggies and dip, cheese cubes, deli crackers, chips and salsa, and any of your other favorites.

For extra fun, give your late-night buffet a theme. You could go Mexican and decorate the table with sombreros, colorful confetti, and lots of yummy Mexican food. Then, fill a piñata with candy and let each guest take a shot at it. Or have a Chinese buffet and give each friend a fortune cookie filled with words of wisdom. No matter what foods or theme you plan, you'll have a blast.

Okay then—ladies, gentlemen—tie on your bibs!

89

❧

BECOME THE
ANSWER TO
SOMEONE'S
PRAYER

S o many prayers to answer—how does God do it? Very often He uses people just like you: people whose hearts are open to hear Him and whose hands are willing to do His work.

Of course, some requests are beyond our capabilities and many God has not asked us to answer. But there are other prayers prayed every day by people who need a kind word, a smile, a hand up, someone to talk to, someone to care. If you're willing, God will use you to answer those prayers.

It won't take long for you to learn to hear God's voice speaking to you, guiding you, showing you those in need. But while you're learning, try this simple strategy:

Each morning, spend some time—five to ten minutes is more than enough—praying for your own needs for the day. As you pray, write the items you've prayed for on a small slip of paper. Maybe you need encouragement, help with a particular school subject, cooperation from the members of a committee you're heading. When you're through, go down the list, thanking God for an answer for each item and asking Him to let you help someone else in the same way He is helping you. Put the paper in your pocket and carry it with you through the day.

Then open your eyes to really see each person you meet. Do you see discouragement? Speak kind and gracious words of encouragement. Do you see someone who is struggling with a subject you're good at? Offer to share your understanding. Do you see someone who needs cooperation to carry out a responsibility? Pitch in and give it your all.

As you become the answer to others' prayers, you will see your own prayers quickly answered.

90

ENTER A
WRITING
CONTEST

W hether you're pursuing a career in marketing, engineering, or business, good writing skills are essential. Just read through the career classified ads and you'll know that's the truth. Almost every ad says, "Strong verbal and writing skills required." Employers want their associates to be able to compose strong letters, effective e-mails, and clear and concise reports—no matter what their job description.

So what better way to boost your résumé than to add "Writing contest winner"? And let's face it, you've probably written enough reports, essays, and poetry to fulfill academic requirements that you have some good stuff just lying around, waiting to be entered!

Whether you like to write poetry, historical essays, short stories, or songs, there is a writing contest for you. You just have to know where to find it. First, check out campus competitions. Your school may sponsor various opportunities to wield your pen, so ask your academic advisor. Also, look for opportunities in the Lifestyle section of your city's newspaper. Around Valentine's Day, you may find requests to write about your first love or your worst date ever. (You're thinking of that story right now, aren't you?)

Whichever contest you choose, don't be afraid to give it a try. You never know—you just might win!

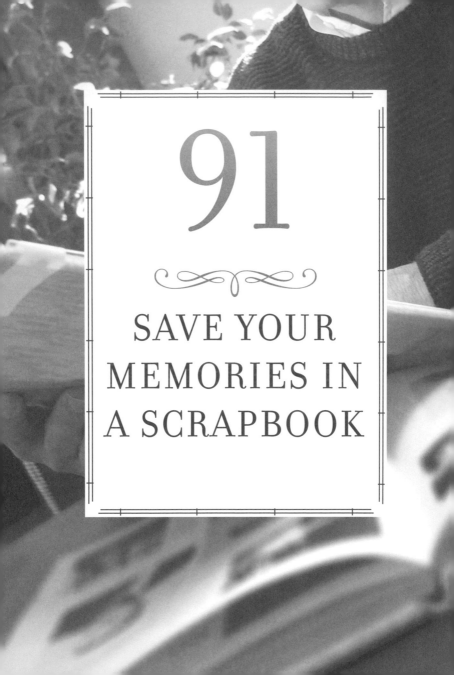

91

SAVE YOUR
MEMORIES IN
A SCRAPBOOK

Right now you probably think you won't miss a thing about school. The sooner you can flip that tassel and snatch that diploma from the hand of the presiding dignitary the better. You plan on walking off that stage and never looking back. One day, though, you will look back—fondly. That's when you'll be glad you took some time to save your memories.

An entire industry is devoted to helping you do just that. Remember these important tips:

1. Shop for the items you need at a store that specializes in scrapbooking, which will have everything you need in one location.

2. Choose supplies (album, paper, plastic sheeting, etc.) labeled "Photo Safe." This means the material is acid free and will not destroy your photographs.

3. Invest in a photo-labeling pencil. This is a special pencil that allows you to write on the front and back of your photographs without damaging them. The writing will wipe off with a cotton ball or tissue.

4. Use a spray neutralizer to coat items like ticket stubs, programs, and other memorabilia. This will deacidify the items.

5. Add a personal touch by journaling your thoughts and describing the details surrounding each item.

Even if scrapbooking is a bit of a stretch for you—listen up, guys—you should still make an effort to preserve your memories. Find a wooden box and use it to store your valuables, things like sports letters, fraternity rings, ticket stubs, newspaper articles chronicling your achievements, even love letters from someone special. Your memories will increase in value with each passing day. Make sure you take yours with you when you go.

92

❦

ENJOY
SOMEONE
ELSE'S MUSIC

W ho can explain why one person likes rap and another likes jazz, while someone else likes pop? Some of it is tied to culture, some to age, but for the most part, it's a matter of exposure. We tend to have mind-sets about musical genres. Classical is stuffy, rap lyrics are obscene, jazz is boring, pop is juvenile and overly emotional, gospel is too preachy and overbearing. Country is too whiny. Rock is loud and obnoxious.

The truth is that just like the people who listen to it, music cannot be stereotyped. Unless you're willing to try a little or even a lot, you could be missing out on a pleasing sound for a lifetime.

It isn't necessary to switch completely to something else, even for a time. But you can try this simple experiment: Ask friends what their favorite radio stations are or what songs they would recommend to add to your playlist. Listen once a day for a week and let the music move past your protective prejudice and penetrate your mind. Listen to the words, hear the instrumentals, pick up on the rhythms. Close your eyes and let it in.

After engaging in this experiment, you may still not like some types of music. That's all right. Chances are, however, that you've made some startling discoveries. *The William Tell Overture* is really a lot of fun. Elvis has the voice of an angel. Certain country singers make you want to stamp your feet and say, "Yeehaw!"

As with anything else in life, you must step outside your comfort zone in order to live fully. Expand your musical territory and you'll expand your world.

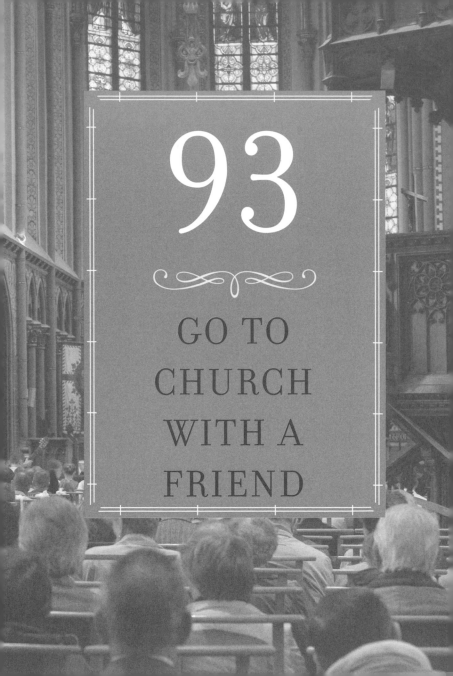

93

GO TO
CHURCH
WITH A
FRIEND

I f you've been going there for a while, your church home probably feels all comfy-cozy. You know the people, and they know you. The music suits you, the service is familiar, the preacher's style is suitable to your tastes. You're set! Well, yes . . . except you might be in heaven before you realize there's more than one way to worship God. Take a Sunday now and then and visit someone else's place of worship. It could be an invigorating and heartwarming experience.

Don't misunderstand—church-hopping is not a sport. It's best to be settled in a church, systematically learning about Him and His Word, being accountable to the other believers in terms of your spiritual growth. But He also wants you to understand that you and your little band of believers by no means represent the entirety of His presence on the earth. He's eager for you to see that His body cannot be confined to any church building or limited by any man-made structure. His ways surpass the heartiest processes, most ironclad doctrines, and all grandiose endeavors. God cannot be put in a box and neither can His church.

Ask a friend if you might go to church with him or her one week. Observe and participate in their rituals, sing the songs they hold dear, listen with your heart to the message, and meet the people (fellow brothers and sisters in Christ). The experience will do you good. It will help you better grasp the concept of the universal church and appreciate your own group of believers' special strengths. Venture outside—briefly—and have a look around. It will be good for your soul.

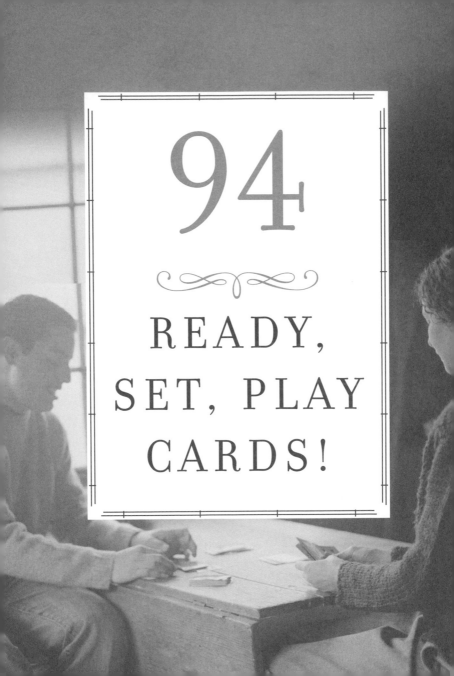

94

READY,
SET, PLAY
CARDS!

A deck of cards looks like a pretty boring pastime: No graphics. No handheld controls. No sound effects. No batteries or extension cords. Just a stack of fifty-two plastic-coated pieces of paper. But before you discount playing cards as a hobby for old folks or magicians-in-training, consider this: people around the world have been playing cards for over six hundred years. A fad like that has got to have something going for it! The only way you can find out what the fuss is all about is through a little hands-on experience of your own.

Hearts. Pinochle. Go Fish. Rummy. Solitaire. War. A deck of cards isn't limited to one kind of game. Games have been invented for all ages and attention spans. Ask your friends to teach you any card games they know. Ask your parents, or even your grandparents, what they enjoy playing. You may be surprised to find how versatile a game of cards can be when it comes to building social interaction, making friends, stimulating brain cells, and engaging in friendly competition. Why—it's golf, without all the expense, equipment, time commitment, and obsessive behavior!

Playing cards can help you settle your mind, release your anxiety, and think through difficult situations. And you can play with them anywhere from your kitchen table to a campsite in the woods to a seat on a plane. Better yet, a deck of cards never breaks down. The only power it requires comes from your own brain. The next time the words "I'm bored" begin to echo through your head, pick up a deck and deal.

95

GET UP IN
TIME TO SEE
THE SUN RISE

As a student, you know all about what early mornings are like. Five days a week your alarm clock jars you to consciousness long before you're ready to face another day. So when the weekend or (Oh joy! Oh bliss!) a holiday break rolls around, the thought of getting up to watch the sunrise sounds about as appealing as taking a class in advanced calculus "just for fun." But there's a surprise in the sunrise that you may be missing. That surprise is the whisper of God.

When the day is fresh and new, when the first rays of sun sprint across the horizon in banners of pinks and golds, God's promise of a brand new start seems to echo from the clouds. It's like hope, made visible, sent straight from heaven. And it seems to burn brightest with the dawn, when everything is dew-covered and still, waiting on tiptoe for the day to begin.

Give it a try. At least once. Set your alarm about ten minutes before the sun will rise. Then grab a blanket and plant yourself in front of a picture window or out in your backyard, anywhere where you can get an unhindered view. Take a moment or two to brush the sleep out of your eyes and ask God to help you hear Him. Then, think about God's words in Psalm 118: "This is the day the LORD has made; let us rejoice and be glad in it."

Be as still as the world around you. Ask God to remind you of your reasons to rejoice. Then listen for His gentle reply in your heart. Beginning the day with rejoicing allows joy to spill over into every waking hour. It can change your morning rush into morning refreshment.

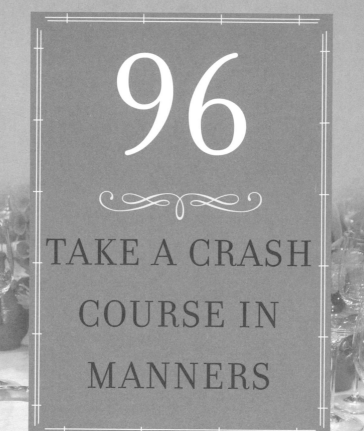

96

TAKE A CRASH COURSE IN MANNERS

S tudents have a reputation for sporting an attitude. The stereotypical student is portrayed as self-centered, unappreciative, and often downright rude—at least in the movies and on TV. But you're not a character on TV. And you're not a "typical" student. As a matter of fact, there is no such thing. Every individual, no matter what season of life he or she is in, is a one of a kind.

So be original. Choose to mind your manners as you prepare for the world of postgraduation. Practicing a few common courtesies will help you build relationships with others, particularly those who might be leveraging the next step in your journey. You're someone destined to make a difference in this world. Someone whose opinion is worth listening to. Someone who can be trusted with responsibility. Someone who cares for others the way God cares for you.

"Mind your manners" is just another way of saying "respect those around you." Respecting the rights of others is the first step toward gaining the respect of others. Respect gives credit where credit is due. It says "Please" and "Thank you." It drives courteously. It doesn't interrupt conversations but is a careful listener. It not only readily admits mistakes but learns from them. It can ask for forgiveness or accept an apology and still maintain a relationship. It thinks before it speaks or acts. It is generous and patient, courteous and punctual, honest and humble. As a matter of fact, it looks a lot like love.

Long before you graduate, take a good look at how your manners measure up. Act like the person you hope to be and before you know it, you'll be that person: well mannered, well respected, and well on your way to becoming all God created you to be.

97

WEAR WHAT FEELS GOOD

You've got style. It's part of who you are, woven right into your soul. Your own sense of style helps you decide what you'll put on every morning, how you'll wear your hair, and what color becomes your all-time favorite. But sometimes your sense of style can get buried beneath fads and peer pressure and advertising campaigns. Before you graduate, do yourself a favor: make peace with your own personal style.

People who are "slaves to fashion" are dressing for all the wrong people. They are so concerned with what others think that they've forgotten to express who they really are. Be yourself, from the top of your head to the socks and shoes on your toes. Choose what fits your body, your budget, your lifestyle, and your own personality. Wear what suits the weather so being too hot or too cold won't distract you from what you need to accomplish. Wear what's comfortable so you aren't tempted to pull and tug and check yourself out in the mirror throughout the day.

When your wardrobe complements who you are, inside and out, you can stop focusing on what you look like. You can get up, get dressed, and get on with what's really important—living life to the fullest. After all, your clothes may be an outward expression of who you are, but they are not you. They are just fabric, buttons, and zippers. Without you they are nothing but a load of laundry, limp and lifeless. Clothes can never "make" the man or woman. But they can help keep you comfortable while giving others a glimpse of the person you are on the inside.

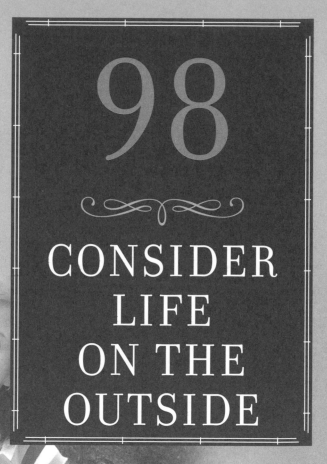

98

CONSIDER LIFE ON THE OUTSIDE

P ut yourself in the doghouse for just a moment—by considering what it would be like to be the family pooch. You spend all day in the house or the yard, just itching for the opportunity to explore the neighborhood on your daily walk. When that chance finally arrives, you tug and pull at the leash. There's so much to see and do! But one day, someone leaves the gate open and you make a break for it. Freedom calls!

You have a new leash on life. You run helter-skelter through the neighborhood, knocking over trash cans and running in front of speeding cars. Before you know it, you're busted: back home with a dog toy and broken dreams. If only you'd had a plan! If only you'd run straight to the bus station, used your savings to purchase a ticket, and headed to Miami where you could fulfill your dream of teaching others how to play Frisbee on the beach!

Okay, so dogs don't have what it takes to plan for the future. But you do. Soon you're going to find yourself outside the family gate, facing freedom in a way you never have before. Before that moment of truth arrives, think long and hard about what kind of life you picture yourself living. Learn a few necessary life skills, like how to balance a checkbook, read a rental agreement, keep your car maintained, get regular health checkups, and whip up a great meal on a tight budget. Make a plan for how you're going to get from where you are today to where you want to go tomorrow.

Why go barking up the wrong tree when freedom calls your name after graduation? A little prayerful planning today can help make your future feel like a walk in the park.

99

❦

HOWL AT
THE MOON

When do you become a bona fide free agent? Is it the day you get your driver's license? Experience your first kiss? Get your first job? Receive your diploma? Many cultures around the world have specific ways in which they mark this special occasion with customs such as withholding food, getting a tattoo, or being abandoned in the wilderness. Aren't you glad you live where you do? (Well, you may want that tattoo, but that's another story!)

Becoming truly independent is cause for celebration. Not that you won't miss some of the fun and freedom you had in childhood and adolescence, when your problems were someone else's problems too. But independence has its own kind of fun. And you can't fully enjoy what's ahead until you leave what's behind, behind.

Even before you are no longer claimed a dependent on your parents' tax return, you can celebrate your own independence day. That's the day you make a conscious choice to wholeheartedly embrace the adventure of maturity. It's the day you say okay to taking responsibility for your own life, your own choices. Becoming mature doesn't mean becoming boring—or trading in your jeans and video games for a suit and a briefcase. It simply means owning your life, for better or for worse.

So choose wisely, beginning today. Mark your decision with your own individual rite of independence. Howl at the moon. Release a balloon into the sky. Donate your childish possessions to a charity. Write a poem. Draw a portrait of yourself. Start a journal. Give yourself a new name—known only to God and you. Whatever you choose to do, mark the day in your own unique way. A brand-new adventure has begun.

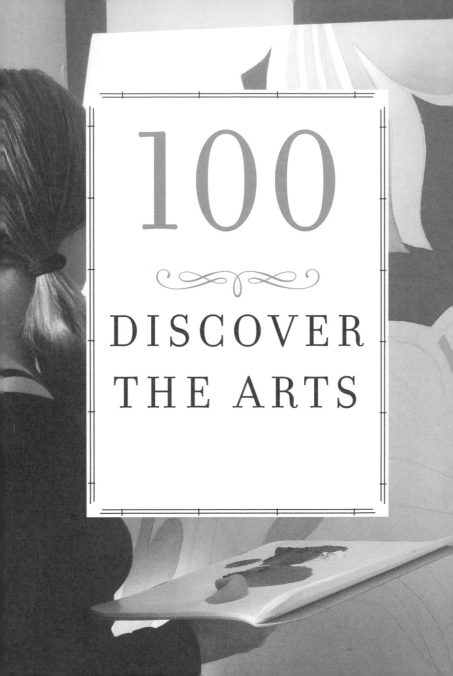

100

DISCOVER
THE ARTS

A rt rocks. It's what gives drum solos power, makes Mona Lisa smile, and ensures that your favorite fairy tales will end with "happily ever after." Art doesn't have a specific job, like a can opener or a forklift. It's something that's almost beyond description. It's an expression of emotion that goes deeper than words. It's an act of creation that points to something more powerful and permanent in this world than what is seen at first glance.

All you have to do is take a good look at the world around you to see that God is the ultimate Artist. The good news is that you are created in His image. That means you share some of His characteristics, like being able to love, to know right from wrong, and to create. You have an artist's heart, just as He does.

Some people are especially gifted in being able to express their "artist's heart" in ways that follow in the creative footsteps of their heavenly Father. They paint. They sculpt. They compose music. They play an instrument. They sing, dance, act, write, scrapbook, sew, knit, or take amazing photographs. Not everyone is gifted in the same way or in the same measure. But each and every person has the potential to express him- or herself in an artistic way.

Have you found your artistic niche? To discover the true power and pleasure of the arts, you need to uncover the hidden artist in yourself. Enjoying movies, jamming along with your MP3 player, coordinating a great outfit, decorating the ultimate Christmas cookie—all of these things can be clues to your artistic expression. Pick up a musical instrument, a paintbrush, a pen, or a lump of clay and begin an art project just for God. Consider it a "thank you" gift for the great art gallery of the world He's shared with you.

101

~

BECOME A
TREASURE
HUNTER

What do you want to be when you grow up? You've probably been asked that question more times than you can count, especially as you get closer to graduation day. But the question's an important one. Your answer will help set the direction for your future. But regardless of whether you choose to become a butcher, a baker, or a candlestick maker, there's another occupation you need to choose to major in. You need to become a treasure hunter.

There's priceless treasure to be discovered in this life—and the next. It can't be found in how much bling you've got in your jewelry box or how many zeros are recorded at the end of your net worth. Becoming a doctor or a rock star won't ensure you find it. But once you've gotten hold of this great treasure, it can't ever be lost or taken away. Not even death can separate you from it.

In the Bible, a story is told about this kind of treasure. It tells of a pearl merchant who searches everywhere to find a pearl that outshines all others. When he finds it, he sells everything he owns to acquire it. The merchant knows the value of what he's found and that his life could never again feel complete without it. That "pearl" is your relationship with God. It's the key that unlocks a treasure chest of joy, purpose, and contentment in your life, as well as the gates of heaven itself.

What do you want to be? What you choose to do will never be as important as who you choose to be. Choose to be the person God created you to be, someone who is dearly loved, graciously gifted, and endlessly blessed. With God by your side, your future can't be anything other than rich and bright.

THOUGHTS OF JOY FOR
LIFE'S JOURNEY

Unless you try to do something
beyond what you have already mastered,
you will never grow.
RONALD E. OSBORN

Opportunity woos the worthy, shuns the unworthy.
Prepare yourself to grasp opportunity, and opportunity is likely
to come your way. It is not so fickle, capricious, and
unreasoning as some complain.
B. C. FORBES

Each honest calling, each walk of life, has its own elite,
its own aristocracy based on excellence of performance.
JAMES BRYANT CONANT

BEFORE I GRADUATE,
I'D LIKE TO . . .

_____

_____

_____

_____

_____

_____

_____

_____

_____

_____

_____

_____

_____

_____

_____

_____

_____

_____

THOUGHTS OF JOY FOR LIFE'S JOURNEY

Live your life each day as you would climb a mountain. An occasional glance toward the summit keeps the goal in mind, but many beautiful scenes are to be observed from each new vantage point. Climb slowly, steadily, enjoying each passing moment; and the view from the summit will serve as a fitting climax for the journey.

HAROLD B. MELCHART

Every moment of this strange and lovely life from dawn to dusk is a miracle. Somewhere, always, a rose is opening its petals to the dawn. Somewhere, always, a flower is fading in the dusk.

BEVERLEY NICHOLS

We should live each day with a gentleness, a vigor, and a keenness of appreciation which are often lost when time stretches before us in the constant panorama of more days and months and years to come.

HELEN KELLER

BEFORE I GRADUATE,
I'D LIKE TO . . .

THOUGHTS OF JOY FOR LIFE'S JOURNEY

To laugh often and much;
To win the respect of intelligent people,
and the affection of children;
To earn the appreciation of honest critics,
and endure the betrayal of false friends;
To appreciate beauty;
To find the best in others;
To leave the world a bit better,
whether by a healthy child, a garden patch,
or a redeemed social condition;
To know that even one life has breathed easier because you lived.
This is to have succeeded.

RALPH WALDO EMERSON

To live only for some future goal is shallow.
It's the sides of the mountain that sustain life, not the top.

ROBERT M. PIRSIG

BEFORE I GRADUATE,
I'D LIKE TO . . .

THOUGHTS OF JOY FOR LIFE'S JOURNEY

Most of us miss out on life's big prizes. The Pulitzer. The Nobel. Oscars. Tonys. Emmys. But we're all eligible for life's small pleasures. A pat on the back. A kiss behind the ear. A four-pound bass. A full moon. An empty parking space. A crackling fire. A great meal. A glorious sunset. Hot soup. Don't fret about copping life's grand awards. Enjoy its tiny delights. There are plenty for all of us.

ADVERTISEMENT FOR UNITED TECHNOLOGIES CORPORATION

*Start by doing what's necessary,
then what's possible, and suddenly you are doing the impossible.*

SAINT FRANCIS OF ASSISI

*The great thing in the world is not so much where we stand,
as in what direction we are moving.*

OLIVER WENDELL HOLMES

BEFORE I GRADUATE,
I'D LIKE TO . . .

THOUGHTS OF JOY FOR LIFE'S JOURNEY

The Things We Can't Afford

We can't afford to win the gain
That means another's loss;
We can't afford to miss the crown
By stumbling at the cross.

We can't afford the heedless jest
That robs us of a friend;
We can't afford the laugh that finds
in bitter tears an end.

We can't afford to play with fire
Or tempt a serpent's bite.
We can't afford to think that sin
Brings any true delight.

We can't afford with serious heed
To treat the cynic's sneer.
We can't afford to wise men's words
To turn a careless ear.

But blind to good are we apart
From Thee, all-seeing Lord;
O grant us light that we may know
The things we can't afford.

AUTHOR UNKNOWN

BEFORE I GRADUATE,
I'D LIKE TO . . .